KINESICS:
THE POWER OF SILENT COMMAND

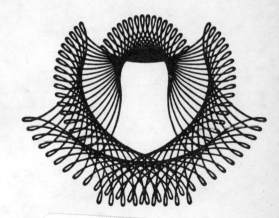

D0487116

THORSONS

MERLYN CUNDIFF

THORSONS PUBLISHING GROUP

First published in the United Kingdom 1980
This edition published 1989

Original American edition published by
Parker Publishing Company, West Nyack, New York

A CIP catalogue record for this book is available
from the British Library

ISBN 0-7225-2234-7

*Published by Thorsons Publishing Group,
Wellingborough, Northamptonshire, NN8 2RQ, England.*

Printed and bound in Great Britain by
Mackays of Chatham PLC, Chatham, Kent

3   5   7   9   10   8   6   4   2

What This Book Can Do for You

In the next few minutes you are going to start to discover the secret of Silent Command — a secret so startling that it may change your life forever. You are about to learn how to unleash a titanic force that now sleeps within you — the force of KINESICS!

Actually, KINESICS is the oldest form of communication known to man. It is used by animals, birds, fish — even certain plants. And once you learn how it works, you can put this secret to work for you to achieve all the power, wealth, influence, and control over people you've ever wanted.

All of this is possible through a series of recent discoveries by America's greatest mind scientists. They have probed, tested, experimented, and studied this phenomenon for many years. Some have called it "body language" . . . others refer to it as "non-verbal communication" . . . "body communication" . . . "kinesics" . . . "persuasive communication" . . . and by many similar terms. All of these terms are identical, and I have used them interchangeably throughout this book.

The Secret of Silent Command

Once you have mastered the simple techniques of KINESICS . . . once you discover how to read people like a book, to know what they are thinking without their saying a word . . . you are ready for the next step: SILENT COMMAND.

Simply by standing or sitting in a certain way, by moving certain parts of your body in subtle ways, or by the other methods described in this book, you will find that you can project unspoken orders that must be obeyed.

"Does this power really exist?" you ask. And the answer is startling almost beyond belief. Not only does this power exist — but certain people are using it right now to win vast rewards and influence others. Perhaps someone is even using it to control YOU. Now the time has come to turn the tables!

This Book a Road Map to Your Goal

The purpose of this book is to show you the way . . . to give you a "psychic road map" that will guide you from where you are now to where you want to be . . . to bridge the gap between what you have and what you want.

In order to do this, you need only learn a few simple rules . . . some easily-mastered basic techniques . . . and find out when and how to apply them. There's no need to spend long hours doing this — if you are willing to spend just five minutes a day, the power of Silent Command can be yours.

Why Kinesics Must Work a Miracle for You

Kinesics is guaranteed to work for you — and so is Silent Command. Why? Because they have already worked for thousands of men and women in all walks of life. These men and women are no richer, no smarter, no better-educated than you are — but they all have one thing in common: a burning desire to better themselves. If — like them — you're not satisfied with just "half a loaf" . . . if — like them — you want the expensive clothes; the big, high-priced new cars; the fine mansion in the country; and scores of other luxuries you've been denied too long . . . then this book is for you.

Why should others enjoy the pleasures of life: the adventure of foreign travel, the thrill of leadership, the close friendship of attractive members of the opposite sex, the respect and admiration of everyone you meet, and all the other beautiful things you want ... while you stand aside and eat your heart out? You deserve a full, heaping share of these golden blessings — and, if you follow the techniques I am shortly going to reveal, you will receive them ten times over!

The Simple ... Easy ... Fast Way to What You Want

Before I do, however, there are a few things you must understand. First, these techniques are simple to use. You do not need any special training or advanced education to use them. They have been tried by everyone from grade-school dropouts to college presidents, and have worked just as well for all.

Second, these techniques are easy to use. They require no equipment of any kind, except perhaps a pencil and paper, in some cases, to record your discoveries. Of course, if you have other equipment, you can certainly use it. A tape recorder may be handy for helping you pick up the techniques of Kinesics faster, for example. But I want to emphasize that you don't *need* such devices. All you need is a sincere desire to improve your life.

Third, these techniques work rapidly once you start to use them. In just a few minutes, you can see the innermost thoughts and desires of everyone you come in contact with, just as if they were written in indelible ink on their foreheads. You don't have to *guess* what others think about you, you *know*. You don't have to *wonder* what they really want from you, you *know*. And you don't have to *hope* you'll say the right thing every time, you *know*. You can't fail — because no one can have any secrets from you!

Some Amazing Results of "Silent Command"

In this book, you'll see how:

- A 73-year old woman used the secret of Silent Command to close a sale for $18,000,000.00.

- The movement of a spoon for two inches turned hostility between a man and a woman into a friendly, relaxed situation.
- A speaker took off his eyeglasses, and made his audience go wild with applause.
- A professor's "hot button" was pressed, and he immediately expressed his feelings with great passion.
- A doctor who "radiates" a certain attitude can become the leading doctor in his city.
- A man invites a beautiful woman to join him without saying a word.

   ... and many other instances of how KINESICS and the power of Silent Command worked miracles in the lives of executives, housewives, salesmen, teachers, secretaries, lovers, and other people in every rank of life.

Now — The Amazing Power
of Silent Command Is Yours!

This has been the barest outline of what KINESICS and the power of Silent Command are, and how they can help you. In the pages that follow I am going to go into these things in detail, step by step, so that you will become master of these techniques from A to Z.

Some of these techniques may sound strange to you at first — but all I ask is that you read them and try them with an open mind. Once you see the wonderful results — how others do what you want them to, without your uttering a word — how loved ones come to you without your having to ask — how others start to do unexpected favors for you — and how you begin to command the esteem of friends, family, and fellow-workers almost overnight — then you will finally be convinced.

The Lifetime Plan for
Silent Command Power Development

This book presents what is, in effect, a lifelong plan for the development of your Silent Command power — a plan that strengthens and increases your power over others year after year. It gives you what amounts to an invisible "leash" to lead others with . . . a "psychic whip" that makes others obey you or suffer the consequences. Yet the methods you use are completely honest and ethical, and in no way violate anyone's religious or moral beliefs.

This new power is about to surge into your life. It will change things for the better for you, once and for all. It will shatter the walls that now hem you in, and guide you to some of the most exciting, pleasurable and rewarding experiences of your life.

There is but one word in the Book of Destiny. That word is "NOW!"

Merlyn Cundiff

Table of Contents

What This Book Can Do for You 3

1. Kinesics and Persuasive Communication 17

Simplicity Is Vital — The Complex and the Important
Are Not the Same • Anyone Can Learn to Communicate
• Good Communication Is the Vehicle of Success • How
Much Time Do You Spend Communicating? • Simple
Communication Is a Never-Ending Study • Communica-
tion Conditioning • A New Method of Conditioning •
Kinesics and Silent Command • Don't Learn by Experi-
ence Alone • The Secret of Synthetic Experience

2 How to Get Instant Cooperation from Others 25

Know What You Want to Say • Say It in a Way That
Can Be Understood • First Consider the Respondent •
Watch Your Semantics • Use His Yardstick of Under-
standing, Not Yours • Do Your Homework • How to Be
Flexible in Your Approach • Relating to His Under-
standing Sets Up the Interview • How to Convince
Rather Than Impress • How to Win Instant Acceptance
• Go Over to His Side • The Need for Understanding
Continues • The Need for Understanding on the Job •
How to Bait the Hook • Did You Ever Feel Instant Fail-
ure? • Face Saving Pays Dividends

3. The Amazing "FFF" Technique That
Makes Others Agree 37

The Play Is the Thing • Everyone Loves a Story • How
the FFF Principle Can Convince • Why FFF Is So Important • Imitator or Initiator — Thermometer or Ther-

The Amazing "FFF" Technique That Makes Others Agree (cont.)

mostat • How to Read People's Minds • Third Party Influences • Facts, Analogies and Comparisons Persuade • Get Into the Act • The Ten-Minute Sand Glass Technique • The Empty Envelope Technique • How's Your Story Book Bank Account?

4. The Automatic Way to Get What You Want 45

An Ancient Greek Mind-Probing Technique • Starting the Two-Way Flow • How to Pinpoint the Problem • A Technique That Saves Time • How to Get What You Want Automatically • A Two-Way Interest • Making the Initial Approach • Measure of Value • Sincerity in Communication • The Technique the Professionals Use • The Question Approach • A Simple Test • The Greatest Compliment • What You Have Vs. What You Want • Defining the Problem • Statement Vs. Admission • Controlling the Situation with Silent Command • Shades of Difference in Communication • Getting Time to Think

5. The Psychic Compass That Reveals What Others Desire 57

How to Discover What Others Think • The Inaudible Sound • Creative Listening • The Psychic Compass • Improving the Communication Climate • How to Get the Cue • How to Follow Through on the Cue • Problem Solving Through Listening • Don't Be an Impulsive Respondent • Good Listening Pays Dividends • Why People Don't Listen • How Can We Improve Our Listening Techniques? • How Long Should You Wait Before Answering? • Getting Complete Attention • Improving your Concentration Span • The Empathetic Listening Technique • How to Use the Psychic Compass to Help You

The Secret of Kinesics 67

Triumph or Surrender • Hidden Meanings in Kinesics • Is There a Founder of Kinesics? • Today's Kinesics •

The Secret of Kinesics (cont.)

Kinesics Reveals Local Customs • Body Contact • Kinesics Is an Honest Revelation • What Pupil Widening Means • Painting the Face from the Inside • Pantomiming • Entire Scene in Body Communication • Masked Faces • Like an Old Shoe • A Costume Party • Dropping the Mask • Why Remove the Mask? • Table Positions and Silent Command • Kinesics of a Round Table • Who Picks Up the Tab? • Body Communication Speaks Constantly

7. **Kinesics and Silent Command** 81

How to Read People's Minds with Body Language • The Moment of Truth — How to Spot It • When to Use Silent Command • A Kinesics Technique worth $18,000,000.00 • What Folded Arms Mean • He Wouldn't Ask Me • The King's Protector • What Eyes Reveal • Don't Ignore Shoulders • What Posture Tells You • How to Feel More Confident • How to Listen to Complex Body Language • Avoiding Offense • How to Notice the Small Body Whispers • Hands Over Eyes • Slapping One's Forehead • Fingers Together • Public Kinesics • Drumming Fingers • Foot Signals • Change of Position • Watch for Body Communication

8. **Space Communication and Territorial Invasion** 93

The Territorial Need • Law Recognizes Its Sanctity • Sanctity of Space Transfer • Space Encroachment • The Spoon Episode • A Fascinating Experiment • The Mental Satisfaction of Space • The Deepest Human Need • Please Keep Your Distance • Mental Halitosis • The Privacy Zone • How Distance Communicates Respect • The Appearance of Intimacy • The Big-Top Table • Violating Zone Barriers

9. **How to Listen with Your Eyes** 103

Reading Others' Minds • Visual Listening Reliable • Verbal Vs. Visual Communication • Convincing Actions • Less Say — More Do • Use This Tested Technique • Why Some People Get Hired and Others Don't • Lis-

How to Listen with Your Eyes (cont.)

tening with Your Subconscious • Your "Sixth Sense" and How to Use It • How to Turn On Your Magic Communicator • 20-20 Communication Vision • Employment Vision • How to Impress an Interviewer • Body Language Is a Two-Way Street • The Casual Friendly Approach • Getting Attention with Gimmicks • Three Miracles of Body Communication • The Invisible Barometer • How to Take Calculated Risks

10. How to Project Unspoken Orders That Must be Obeyed 115

Your Psychic Road Map • Secret of Structured Thinking • How to Move People to Action • Basic Formula for Action • The Crasher Technique • Basic Selling Technique • The Third Dimension Technique • Selecting the Right Method • The Cundiff 4-Ply System • The First Step • How to Make Others See Things Your Way • The Cloak and Dagger Technique • The Second Step • The Subjective Sale Technique • The Third Step • How to Offer Proof That Convinces • The "Q" Technique • The Fourth Step • How to Ask for Action • Refusal Is Not Rejection • Don't Fear Fear • Built-In Vince Lombardi • How to Overcome Objections Quickly • The Only Action That Counts • Step-by-Step Control Plan • Physical Interview • Mental Interview • Emotional Interview

11. Preventing Communication Breakdowns 129

Take Out Insurance on Good Communication • Case Study • Showing the Entire Picture • How to Increase Understanding • Diminishing Understanding • The Colonel's Command • Garnishing the Story • How to Get the Best Support from Others • Improving Efficiency • How to Add Value • Just a Fragment of the Picture

12. The Vital Secret of Silent Command 137

How to Build Up Others • Convincing Others Without Effort • The Cruelest Thing to Do • Discovery Applies to All Fields • Another Key Principal • How to Communicate Objectively — Not Subjectively • Five Words

The Vital Secret of Silent Command (cont.)

of Power • How to Get the Decision You Want • "Low Pressure" Influencing • Mental Television Broadcasting • How to Make People Pay Attention to You • Controlling the Communication Climate • The Message in the Eyes • The Ego Complex • How to Create Confidence in You

13. **Unleashing the Ultimate Power of Silent Command ... 147**

ITA VS. ICA • How a Doctor Becomes Rich • The Miracle That Takes Only a Few Seconds • The Remarkable Sign • This Sign Is Always There • Volcanic Spirits • The Great Idea • The Magic Key That Opens All Doors • A Rare Opportunity • The Masked Men Who Failed • The Ultimate Consumer • Searching the Soul • The Kinesics of the Reception Room • What Does Your Appearance Communicate? • How to Please a Woman • Ready and Willing • The Exalted Look

14. **Getting Cooperation in Business Through Silent Command 157**

Secrets of Effective Company Meetings • When to Hold the Meeting • How to Plan the Meeting Strategy • How to Cover the Vital Points • Proper Direction of the Meeting • How to Open the Meeting • How to Maintain Control of the Meeting • Duty of the Chairman • Following Up • Incentive Policies • Training New People • How to Get Maximum Performance • Reviewing and Evaluating Work • What Is the Yardstick in Judging Me? • Making People Feel Involved • How to Fire People Without Bitterness • Giving Instruction Attractively • Examples of Good and Bad Communication • Overworked • Where to Put the Files • Old-Fashioned Method •Not My Responsibility • How Urgent? • I Don't Like the Program • The Six Most Useful Words for Supervisors

15. **How to Handle Specific Situations with Silent Command 169**

How to Introduce a Speaker • Importance of the Subject • Particularly Important to This Audience • Espe-

**How to Handle Specific Situations
with Silent Command (cont.)**

cially Qualified Speaker • A Model Introduction • Prostituting an Introduction • The Rule of Brevity • The Element of Surprise • Relationship Between Chairman and Speaker • Platform Kinesics • How to Present a Trophy or Plaque • Four Points of the Presentation • Example of Presentation • How to Accept a Trophy or Plaque • The Use of Exhibits • How to Reveal an Exhibit • Appearance and Disappearance • How to Build Up the Exhibit's Importance • How to Use Notes • Handling Notes on the Platform • How to Give Prestige to a Speech • Substitute Mental Notes

**16. The Lifetime Plan for Silent Command
Power Development** 185

On Waking Up • Stoplights and Go-Lights • Starting with the Right Attitude • Secret of Controlled Excitement • Take This Simple Test • An Ancient Doctrine • The Blind Spots • Radiation of Emotions • Understanding Your Duties • How to Avoid Being a Victim • The Perfect "Out". • The Most Effective Tool • An Intriguing Motivator • Benefits Not Features • The Great Difference • Appointment Vs. Interview • The Presentation • Profitable Difficulty • The Blessings of Being Sensitive • The Twin Factors You Need to Win • Insulation Against Rejection • Restoration a Necessity • The Only Answer • Continuous Motivation • The Master Secret

17. The Kinesics of Courtship and Romance 199

Courtship Signals in Animals and Men • Using the Power of Sex Communication • Communication by Dress • Color Communicating • Persuasion Through Odor • Using Eye Communication • The Come-Hither Look • The "I Am Willing" Stare • The Extent of Intimacy • How to Make an Appointment with Your Eyes • Communication by Voice Pitch • Body Position • The Language of Sexual Communication

18. The Rewards of Silent Command **211**

A Great Inventor's Secret • An Action Plan for Daily Living • How to Get Help When You Need It • How to Prepare for the Future • The Two-Edged Sword • The Second Question • The Amazing Rewards of Silent Command • The Greatest Gift • The Magic Formula • No Limits to Your Success • The Day of the Flying Clock • New Worlds to Conquer • How to Become a Leader • You Shall Be the Miracle • The Secret of Lifelong Improvement • Today Is Your Day! • The Supreme Challenge • Opportunity Is Everywhere • You Cannot Fail

ONE

Kinesics and Persuasive Communication

Regardless of what else you derive from this book, please master the three primary rules of effective, persuasive communication:

1. Be *simple* in your presentation.
2. *Relate* your presentation to the other person's understanding.
3. Tell stories and give generous "for instance's."

We shall devote a whole chapter to each of these principles. In fact, throughout this entire book we shall refer again and again to these three cardinal rules that insure persuasion and understanding.

Simplicity Is Vital — The Complex and the Important Are Not the Same

Today, too often we confuse the complex with the important. We think that because something is important it also must be presented in a complex manner. We forget the divinity of simplicity.

I once heard someone say that if the safety pin had been invented in this generation no one would use it unless it had six moving parts, two transistors, and required servicing twice a year.

Anyone Can Learn to Communicate

Never forget this truth: Anyone who can talk or write can learn to communicate effectively if he will only follow certain basic principles.

The answer does not lie in any intricate formula; the solution is not contained in any hidden secret. In fact some might feel that the pattern is too obvious to need elaboration, too simple to need an explanation. I would agree completely, except for the fact that so few people follow this simple pattern.

Reduced to the lowest common denominator, persuasive communication is just this simple:

> First, you must know just what you want to say, and second, you must say it in a convincing way, which can be understood by others.

Because of the utter simplicity of the principle, people fail to realize that they must keep studying its applications. The idea is so simple it seems insignificant.

Many people feel that the art of persuasion can be mastered only by the person who sells a product or service, and that this art is only useful to salespeople. This is certainly not true. Everybody, regardless of what work he does, needs to be persuasive. Unless a person can sell himself through good communications, he will never advance or get ahead in life. No matter what your occupation is, you must learn to communicate in a persuasive way.

A noted industrialist recently made the remark that there is no phase of our economic life more neglected, in the light of its importance, than improving the ability of the average person in business to communicate. In business particularly, ability to communicate is extremely important in passing along the lessons of experience and in preventing mistakes. A teacher I once had would often say, "Don't keep mopping the floor; turn off the faucet!" He then would elaborate on the colossal insanity of spending so much time correcting mistakes that never should have occurred in the first place.

Today we have a whole new philosophy in the medical

field called preventive medicine. In the industrial safety field we have a similar philosophy known as accident prevention. Yes, in every field of endeavor today it is recognized that the only intelligent approach to our problems is found in preventive measures rather than expensive correction after the harm is done.

In no facet of our economic life is this principle more important than in the field of communication. A corporate president recently told me that if his company could only have prevented certain mistakes that never should have been made in the first place, the company's earnings during the past year would have been more than double. But then he went on to give the startling fact that these mistakes did not arise from a lack of company know-how but had their origin in lack of communication.

Good Communication Is the Vehicle of Success

The most valuable ore deposits of this world would lie worthless and unmined if there were no method of bringing them to the smelter. The richest forests would be of little industrial value unless there were facilities to bring the lumber to the mill.

The same principle holds true in communication. Regardless of how well informed you may be on any subject or in any field, unless you can transmit this information to others, it will remain, like the rich deposits of metal in the earth and the valuable lumber in the forest, of no value to anyone.

So let's start with the major premise that we can only bring our wares to market, yes, only cash in on our potentials, through persuasive communication.

How Much Time Do You Spend Communicating?

The average businessman today spends the greater part of his working hours engaged in communication. Salesmen and public relations people spend an even greater part of their time communicating with others. Consider for a moment your own case. Just how important is the art of communication to you?

Why are we so loath to spend the time necessary to prepare ourselves for this important endeavor? Think how much the productivity of our efforts would be increased if we could only improve our communication by ten per cent! The increased results added up over a whole year would be staggering.

Simple Communication Is a Never-Ending Study

Regardless of what line of endeavor a person follows he should always be studying and practicing to be a more persuasive communicator. School is never out for the person who wants to be a professional in making himself felt, heard and understood.

Constant study is important, not only because of the vast never-ending scope of this subject, but also because the meanings of words and phrases are constantly changing. No person can train himself in communicating and then simply stop studying.

A word which has a definite meaning today might suggest something else five years hence and have an entirely different meaning ten years from today. How much meaning do you think the words "jet-propelled," "ecology," "fall-out" or "computerized" would have had to the very best informed person of the twenties?

Communication Conditioning

It is important to realize that it is not enough to know the meaning of words or even to have an academic grasp of certain knowledge.

Until we so completely *condition* ourselves to these words and to this knowledge that we feel comfortable in their use, we cannot profit by such new acquisition to any extent

A New Method of Conditioning

It is reported that the average salesman spends six years of his life today driving around in his automobile. He spends three years of his life dressing, shaving and preparing for work. He spends a comparable amount of time eating his meals. Wouldn't it be a great savings of time and also a great training experience if he could use some of this time to condition himself for better communication?

There are on the market today little cassette recorders which sell for as low as $20.00. These little recorders can be carried in our car or used while dressing and eating. They offer a wonderful opportunity for conditioning ourselves in any field of learning, and whether we are salespeople or not, they can help us condition ourselves for better communication.

I keep such a recorder on the seat of my car at all times. I have another in my home. Not only do I have tapes that constantly remind me of the principles of good communication, but I also have tapes that teach me the enunciation of commonly used words which are difficult to pronounce. Unless they could be quickly replaced, I would not sell these recorders and tapes at any price!

Kinesics and Silent Command

You must realize that you do not communicate through words alone. In this book we shall thoroughly cover the science of body communication known as *kinesics*. This is a most fascinating subject and one so important that it's one of the "hottest" things in psychology today.

Very few people realize that they communicate constantly without words. They communicate by the clothing they wear, by the general posture of their bodies, and even by the tone of their voice.

The person who learns to observe and interpret these body gestures has broadened his scope of understanding. The real expert even puts importance on the body whispers. In fact, he listens with his eyes as carefully as he does with his ears. This skill too must be developed through study and practice. It's the basis of all "Silent Command Power."

Don't Learn by Experience Alone

You may think that experience will teach you all you need to know about persuasive communication. Nothing is more misleading in the field of self-improvement than the statement that "experience is the best teacher." Experience is a teacher but the tuition is too high. We can't afford the many mistakes and loss of time that accompany trial and error.

In practically every field of endeavor the average person must be retrained four times in his lifetime. With the fast-moving changes and new adaptations of our economic system today it may soon be six times.

What if you had to retrain yourself four times through trial and error? Even if you lived long enough, you couldn't survive the emotional trauma it would cause.

The Secret of Synthetic Experience

The only time experience is the best teacher is when it is the other person's experience. Today we have the opportunity of learning by synthetic experience, also known as example.

A dog, chicken or horse only learns through its own experience. Man is the only animal that receives a message beyond the grave. We have books, records, cassette tapes, etc. which record the experience of others even in another generation.

I have known people engaged in a certain business for only two or three years who are far more experienced in their work than people who have been engaged in a similar business for thirty years.

Why? Because the person of only two or three years' experience took advantage of other people's experience by reading and studying.

What would you think of the engineering field if each new generation of engineers invented the wheel again? How much success do you think our generation would have had in inventing the computer if we had been restricted to only the knowledge accumulated during our lifetime? How popular would a surgeon be if he used only the knowledge he acquired through his own operations? How successful would a lawyer find himself if he did not take advantage of the knowledge accumulated over the years by other people?

The most expensive schooling anyone can get is from personal failures. This principle is not restricted to any particular endeavor.

If you are a salesman, remember that your customer's office was never intended to be a classroom for trial and error learning. Don't lose sales to get experience. It's not a fair exchange.

If you are a manufacturer, going broke in order to learn the relationship of income and outgo is a pretty expensive price for knowledge you could get from the experience of other manufacturers.

If you are a merchant, learn from the mistakes of other merchants to be sure that you establish proper purchase price and selling price before your inventory is dissipated.

The accumulation of knowledge today is a relay race and not a private event. Accept the baton of experience from the former runner before starting your race in life.

There is something too costly, reckless and devastating about trying to learn through one's own experience alone. It is like suicide, which I once heard someone describe as "the sincerest form of self-criticism." The trouble is that we get an opportunity to be sincere only once. The same person told of the man being hanged who said, "This is going to be a good lesson to me." The poor fellow never profited by his lesson.

Don't try to learn good communication the costly and unprofessional way.

In whatever line of endeavor you follow, you will find you must communicate with others persuasively. Unless you can transmit your ideas to others convincingly, they are about as useless as the proverbial sun dial in the shade.

You'll need to communicate effectively in your social life and in civic affairs just as much as in your business or profession. At a party or other social gathering, have you ever met a man or woman who deprived you of your solitude without furnishing you with company? This is typical of someone who has never learned the basic rules you'll learn in this book.

Don't let yourself fall into this category. Read this book again and again. Make its principles a part of you. Don't be handicapped by the inability to communicate!

TWO

How to Get Instant Cooperation from Others

Just as water cannot rise above its source, we cannot enlighten anyone beyond our own understanding. If we are honest with ourselves, we all shall admit that too often we start speaking without being sure what it is we want to say. I'm sure we all realize that this is a fatal error.

Know What You Want to Say

Form the habit of taking time to see in your mind's eye a clear and articulate picture of what you desire to communicate before speaking or writing. The importance of the information you desire to communicate and the urgency of the situation will determine how much time you can take for this "mental picture," of course.

This thinking and planning can vary from a casual conversation to hours or even days of outlining, writing and rewriting a speech or presentation of major importance. Remember, an advertising agency may take weeks preparing an important ad containing one picture and a few words to communicate a simple idea to the public. Preliminary thinking and planning is a *must* to avoid communication breakdowns.

Say It in a Way That Can Be Understood

In this book we will refer to the one with whom you are trying to communicate as the *respondent*. In various circumstances, your respondent may be an individual, a group, or even an entire audience of hundreds of people. However, this cardinal principle will always apply: Until you have put yourself in your respondent's shoes and adjusted your approach to *his* understanding, not yours, you are not communicating at all. You are only talking to yourself. Remember this corny old adage: Communication is a dance — and it takes two to tango. As you plan what you are going to say, never forget that your very purpose is to persuade and convince the other person. Concentrate on him rather than on yourself. Put yourself in his shoes.

People are not persuaded by what we say but rather by what they understand. In the art of persuasion, if we could only remember that principle, many of the misunderstandings in life could be avoided.

I am sure no one would take issue with the above statement. So let's look at some of the ways of insuring that what is said is related to the respondent's understanding.

First Consider the Respondent

You certainly would not think you could convey a message to a blind man through the sign language. I am sure you would not attempt to engage in oral conversation with a totally deaf person. The utter futility of talking to a person in a language foreign to his would certainly be obvious.

Yet, every day many of us make a communication mistake almost as unforgivable. We use words, phrases and sentences which are not understandable to the person with whom we are talking.

Something we understand today could easily have an entirely different meaning tomorrow because of change in customs or habits. For instance, I heard a girl say the other day that she had a hole in the seat of her stockings. Before the advent of the panty hose this statement would have had no meaning. But I assure you today it is a calculated hazard to any girl's wardrobe.

Watch Your Semantics

A friend of mine, Cavett Robert, recently told me that he took one of his twin daughters to the orthodontist to have her teeth examined.

The dentist took a look at her teeth, frowned, turned to my friend and said, "Your daughter has a traumatic malocclusion."

My friend said that he almost fainted. He thought he was going to lose his little girl.

Why couldn't the orthodontist have used laymen's language and merely said, "Your little girl has a slight over-bite"?

It is unfortunate that the more versed we become in the semantics of our own business or profession the more careful we must be in talking about our business or profession with outsiders. We forget that others are not as familiar with these terms as we are; consequently we are prone to use them in their presence.

Use His Yardstick of Understanding, Not Yours

I was recently waiting in a reception room for an appointment with a person who was engaged in an extensive farming operation.

To pass the time away I was thumbing through a government magazine on raising lettuce. I chanced to come across this statement, "Temperature is an important factor in the ecological optimum of crop development and the consequent exploitation of water and soil resources."

After reading the sentence several times — even writing it — I gave up on it. When the party I was to see finally came out, I handed him the magazine and asked what the mumbo-jumbo meant. He casually looked at it and said, "It means that if the weather is too hot or too cold the crops have a heck of a time."

I can't believe that the farmers, for whom the bulletin was written, would not have been just as confused by such a statement as I was.

Be sure you are on the same thought pattern with your listener.

We all remember the story of the little boy out on the school playground who said to his friend, "I ain't going."

The teacher, overhearing, walked over to him and said, "Don't say that, Johnny — it is 'I am not going, you are not going, she is not going, we are not going, they are not going'."

Johnny looked up and said, "Hey, Teacher, ain't nobody going?"

Any good communicator uses the yardstick of his respondent's understanding in framing his words, phrases and sentences.

Do Your Homework

When I am asked to speak before any group of people, what do you think is my first step? You are right; I must find out all I can about my audience.

A speech which might get a standing ovation from one audience may be destined to utter failure before another audience. This is a lesson which I have learned over the years from some sad experiences which I prefer to forget.

Recently I spoke to a group of telephone employees on a phase of communication. Naturally I could take certain liberties with such an audience that would be fatal in a speech to some other group.

So don't we all agree that first we must do our homework and study our audience to be sure just wherein lies the responsive note? This applies to both individuals and groups.

How to Be Flexible in Your Approach

Not long ago I jointly conducted a seminar on Human Engineering with an associate of mine. We were calling on people of varied professions and businesses to secure registrations.

My associate had over the years made such a habit of putting himself in the other person's shoes that without realizing it he would adapt the vernacular of the person on whom we were calling.

To a doctor he might say, "This course will certainly help to *heal* any communication faults you may have."

To a lawyer he would say, "John, the help you will get from this seminar will be a *sure verdict* in your favor."

Even to a garage man I remember he said, "Tom, I've got a real *puncture-proof* proposition for you."

Once I accompanied a real estate broker who called on a cotton farmer to sell him an apartment house. When the discussion of mortgage payments came around the broker said, "Bill, how many bales of cotton do you have stacked up outside? Do you know, Bill, three of those bales each year will make the mortgage payments?"

Now Bill understood the worth of that cotton and just how much land, expense and effort it took to produce each bale. The broker immediately received an enthusiastic and responsive reaction.

I sincerely believe that if this broker had been talking with a dairyman he would have quoted the mortgage payments in terms of the milk from a certain number of cows.

Relating to His Understanding Sets Up the Interview

Throughout this book we stress the difference between an appointment and an interview. When we are able to arrange a physical meeting with an individual we have secured an appointment. However, not until we have gotten into his mental and emotional presence do we have an interview. We shall repeat this principle over and over for emphasis.

Don't confine the application of this principle exclusively to the sales field. It applies in all cases where we deal with people. It is one of the cardinal principles in the art of persuasion.

I am sure that it is unnecessary to emphasize the fact that the surest way to move from the physical to the mental presence is by relating the conversation to matters which are in the field of the *listener's* understanding and interest.

How to Convince Rather Than Impress

I had occasion to speak to a state real estate association in a neighboring state. At the same convention and on the program was a vice-president of a bank in that state.

I don't doubt that the banker was well versed in financial matters. In fact his credentials were staggering. However, he made no effort to discuss problems from the real estate person's point of view. Everything he presented was from the approach of a banker and he even used the banker's vernacular. Except for the fact that I was sure I was at a real estate convention, his speech would have made me feel that I was at a bankers' seminar.

When the time came for questions the silence was deafening. The speaker had not only failed to give any solutions but he had not even stimulated or provoked any questions.

It was very obvious that this speaker was so concerned with preserving his banking image that there was no rapport whatsoever with his audience. I am sure you have had occasion to sit in an audience and observe a similar fiasco caused by a speaker.

How to Win Instant Acceptance

At this same convention was another banker. The dif ference in the reception of the two men was embarrassing. This second banker started out in a simple down-to-earth fashion, carefully relating to the real estate person's prob- lem at the outset.

As I recall, he made an initial statement something like this: "Fellows, I realize you've got problems, serious problems, and I want you to know that we too are concerned over them. The fact is, your problems are our problems and we want to work with you in finding a solution to them."

So many questions evolved that there was time for only about half of them to be discussed.

Go Over to His Side

Talking in terms of the other person's position applies to every facet of life. Child psychologists tell us that nothing is more frustrating to a small child when he is afraid than to be told to "be a big man." In the first place he is not a big man; he is only a child. When we tell him to be a big man, we are trying to bring him over to our world, one which he is not yet prepared by nature to enter.

How much better it would be, psychologists tell us, if we would try to see *his* point of view and go over to *his* world. Why not try to relate to *his* understanding?

Wouldn't Johnny react much better if we said something like this: "Johnny, I know exactly how you feel because when I was your age I felt exactly the same way. But you know, Johnny, as you grow a little older you'll get over it as I did. In fact you'll look back someday and laugh about it."

Now isn't it obvious that we shall give Johnny more courage and that we shall establish better communication with him when we approach the problem from *his* point of view — not ours?

The Need for Understanding Continues

Johnny goes off to prep school and is homesick. Do you think Johnny would buy the approach; "You are now a man, Johnny, don't be a sissy. You don't want to be tied to your mother's apron strings all your life, do you?"

Actually Johnny is still not a man. He is still a boy, a homesick boy, going away from home for the first time.

Wouldn't an approach such as this be more effective:

"Johnny, it's tough when anyone who appreciates his home and loves his family has to go away for the first time. It would be sad indeed if your home meant so little to you that you wouldn't go through this experience. All of us go through it and it's bad — I remember. However, Johnny, you'll find that you will make new friends, find new interests, and after a week or two, while you'll not forget your home or love it any less, you'll find that this school will become a second home."

The Need for Understanding on the Job

Johnny has finished college and is in a big corporation which has many employees. At times he is bewildered by company policies and other matters that baffle him.

On one occasion Johnny failed to carry out a directive from his superintendent. The order seemed unnecessary to Johnny. He is now face to face with his superintendent and asks why the order was necessary anyway.

What if the superintendent had been concerned only with preserving his image? What if his major concern had been maintaining his authority? What if he had resorted to the old company policy routine, "Johnny, that is company policy and it's not for you, me or anyone else to question?" Would this have been persuasive communication or even good management? It would have solved nothing, only planted the seed for future trouble.

But let's suppose the superintendent communicates with Johnny by mentally going over to Johnny and mentally stepping into Johnny's shoes: "Johnny, it's very understandable that you should wonder about that order. When I first went with the company I felt just as you do now. In fact, it would be unnatural if every new man didn't feel a little bit as you feel. But you know, Johnny, as time went on and I learned more and more about the workings of the company, I realized that orders of this nature were necessary. Just be patient, Johnny, and go along with us and after a while, you, too, as

I did, will realize why it is so important that everyone follows the directives. I'll try to explain to you from time to time why these orders are so vital, although at times they may seem trivial to you."

It wasn't that Johnny really resisted the order, but he had resented the fact that no one had properly communicated with him regarding the purpose of the directives. Now he felt complimented that someone had approached the problem from his point of interest.

How to Bait the Hook

Will Rogers is credited with saying: "When you go fishing you bait the hook, not with what you like, but with what the fish likes. Did you ever taste a worm? Well, it tastes to you perhaps about like your favorite dish tastes to a fish."

A wonderful group of direct salesmen had a convention at Camelback Inn in Scottsdale, Arizona. I spoke at their opening banquet. These were enthusiastic, emotional people — complete extroverts.

My speech was light and entertaining. Purposely I avoided any heavy material. I didn't feel it was necessary to dwell too long on any subject. So I skipped lightly through, enjoying much playback from my audience. Never have I had a speech better received; never have I received more personal satisfaction from speaking.

A week later I spoke in the same room at Camelback, but this time for an engineers' convention. It was a very large convention and there were many people there who were important to my ambitions. In fact there were over 100 heads of companies that put on conventions for their individual companies. I felt sure that I would "wow" this group with the same speech, gaining the same results.

Did You Ever Feel Instant Failure?

Did you ever feel that you were the victim of instant failure? Did you ever suddenly tell yourself that perhaps you were in the wrong line of endeavor?

Those in the audience of engineers who were not looking at me like a tree full of owls had their mental slide-rules measuring my every statement. I felt that I was undergoing the paralysis of analysis.

Yes, I had made the great mistake of not doing my homework. It was the oratorical equivalent of a fumble on the one-yard line. I had neglected to give first consideration to the nature of my audience. I had violated one of the most important rules of good communication. I failed to approach my subject from my audience's point of view.

While a salesman is emotional and thrives on sentiment and generalizations, an engineer is conditioned in his training to analyze carefully, question every statement, and take nothing for granted. While a salesman is easily motivated an engineer fights against emotion because he feels that it warps his judgment.

Fortunately I had the presence of mind, after seeing my predicament, to reverse my approach. I became more analytical. I used comparisons, examples, testimonials, and offered proof of my position on certain matters.

Although this is not my favorite method of presenting my subject matter, to my relief I gradually saw a radical change in my audience. Before long I almost was convinced that they were rendering a verdict in my favor.

I assure you that this experience was very valuable to me. Never again shall I forget that with an audience as with an individual the communication approach must be made from the other person's point of view. Yes, all we say must be related to the other person's interest and understandings.

Face Saving Pays Dividends

Sometimes when we fail to relate our conversation to the other person's understanding we put him in a very embarrassing situation. The average person does not want to indicate that he fails to comprehend for fear he will appear stupid.

Whenever you find that you are attempting to communicate

by using words and examples foreign to your listener's understanding you should immediately accept the fact that you are at fault. You should apologize for your inability to make yourself clear. You should convince your listeners that you, and not they, are to blame. One of the worst offenses that you can commit is to attack another person's mental capacity. Whenever you discover that you have directed the conversation into a field where your listener is ill at ease you should save face for him by immediately directing the conversation to another field where he will find himself more comfortable.

If I had to single out any one chapter of this book and say that it is of greatest importance, I believe I would have to say that it is this chapter. Consider all matters contained herein. Don't be satisfied to read this chapter only once. Read it many times and use it as a reference.

THREE

The Amazing "FFF" Technique That Makes Others Agree

When I revealed to an elderly experienced speaker, who is a friend of mine, my decision to spend the rest of my life traveling the "chipped beef and mashed potato circuit," he replied with something I'll never forget:

"Well, Merlyn," he said, "knowing you as I do, I realize that nothing I say will change your plans. But I want you to remember this. To be successful in this rat race you must look like a girl, act like a lady, think like a man and work like a horse. Furthermore, you must have the wisdom of Solomon, the patience of Job, the strength and endurance of Hercules, and the skin of a rhinoceros."

I paid little attention to his statement, but after speaking over the country, running for airplanes and living out of a suitcase, I am convinced now that my friend was restrained in his observation.

The Play Is the Thing

Many people will buy the first two chapters of this book. They realize that good communication has its very beginning in the essence of simplicity and the approach from the other person's understanding. However, when we say that one must be dramatic, skepticism begins to creep in. Some people feel, "Here is where the dried pablum of academic theory starts. I knew that eventually we would get around to the psychological mumbo-jumbo."

Let's be fair in our approach and reserve our decision until we have completed this chapter.

Shakespeare said, "The play is the thing." In no field or endeavor is this more true than in the field of communication.

Everyone Loves a Story

People from five to 90 have always loved a story. Our introduction to the Bible was through Bible stories. Is there anyone whose early life was not thrilled by Grimm's fairy tales? Is there anyone whose childhood was so neglected that he was not introduced to "Little Red Riding Hood," or "Goldilocks and the Three Bears"?

So don't you see the magic of communication through stories? Any time we can tell a related story we are sure to hit a responsive note. We have guaranteed attention.

Any good story with a hero, a strong conflict, and at last a happy ending is a kind of little drama. Did it ever occur to you that in your effort to persuade others anytime you give an example or a "for instance" you are actually presenting a drama?

> Henry Smith was faced with this same decision. He felt the dilemma you must feel. However, he accepted this offer and look at the tremendous results he experienced.

Now let's analyze the parts of this little story. Henry Smith was the hero. He had a conflict in his mind — should he or should he not go along with this program? He had the foresight and courage to go along and the outcome was a happy ending.

How the FFF Principle Can Convince

For over two decades proponents of effective communication have urged, in both their writings and teachings, that we should generously use the FFF principle.

If I receive an objection or opposition to my position, it takes self-discipline on my part to refrain from impulsively defending myself. All of us know that in the courtroom of our conscience we have only witnesses for the defense. We have a compulsion to justify our stand, even if it means forgetting the other party's position.

Isn't the following a much more intelligent approach? "Mr. Pleasant, I know just how you feel".. (first *F*). "Others have felt exactly that way also".. (second *F*). "But Mr. Pleasant, this is what they have found".. (third *F*).

Why FFF Is So Important

Now let's put the above under the microscope for examination. You *feel* — others *felt* also — but they *found*.

When I tell a person that I know how he feels I am showing him that I am interested in him — in his point of view. His position is recognized. He is not being ignored. People can tolerate being hated easier than being ignored.

Some people might think that the opposite of love is hate. It is not. It is the feeling of being ignored, of simply being treated as though they didn't exist. No one wants to be a non-person.

But when a person realizes that someone has made an effort to understand him, he is highly complimented. He is now conditioned to listen to the other side of the story. In fact he is likely to make a sincere effort to see the other person's point of view. Be sure to do yourself the favor of using these dynamic, highly charged words: "I know how you feel."

Second, when I say that others have felt that way also, I am eliminating any possibility that my prospect might think I consider his position as being stupid or unreasonable.

What reaction do you think I would get if I said something like this in reply to an objection? "If you were not a businessman I would think that you were kidding me." Or, "How you could ever seriously take a position like that simply defeats me."

Certainly you would get a different reaction than you

would get by some such statement as, "It's perfectly understandable why you should feel that way, Mr. Emerson. In fact the last two people who benefited from this program repeated almost your exact words."

Such an answer as this not only relaxes the prospect, but also "saves face" for him.

The second part of the FFF principle can be inflammatory and even explosive unless we treat it with care. Generously use such expressions as "all of us agree"; "I suggest"; "As you know"; "We all feel." Avoid such expressions as "Anybody ought to know"; "Even a child would realize"; "A person with any sense could see."

Yes, I repeat that this second phase of the FFF principle is designed to assure that the listener is not offended.

Now for the important third F. When I say that others have *found* that certain results follow, I am not presenting opinion or controversial matters to cause an argument. I am only presenting a fact that influences. Just the mere fact that others experienced certain results is highly persuasive in itself. It suggests to the prospect the fear of loss. If he does not do as others did, he runs the risk of losing the advantages they enjoyed.

Imitator or Initiator — Thermometer or Thermostat

Ninety-five per cent of the people today are imitators and only five per cent are initiators. The majority of people are like thermometers that simply reflect the surrounding temperature — not like a thermostat that regulates its own temperature.

We should never forget this great communication principle which can be of unparalleled value to us:

> We shall never be able to give a more persuasive presentation than the fact that others did it and are glad they did it!

How to Read People's Minds

Many people delay buying an article or accepting a service simply because they are afraid that it is not the right thing to do.

These people mentally wear a big sign saying "Help me be right." Often they need assurance. They are completely sold on the object or idea, but they are afraid to take a definite stand. Always remember that nothing can eliminate their fear quicker or more certainly than the fact that others took a definite stand and experienced happy results.

Remember, the *feel, felt, found* approach is a great drama. It is insurance and persuasion of the very highest caliber. Avail yourself of this valuable method in every instance possible. Have stories and examples available for every point in your presentation. You may find an occasion to use them at any time. Never let the "cupboard be bare" as far as story illustrations are concerned.

Third Party Influence

In a court of law, if a party to a case testifies in his own behalf, the testimony is considered as a self-serving statement and has very little, if any, influence on the judge or jury. However, if a third party, one who is not in any way interested in either the plaintiff or defendant, gives the same testimony, such evidence is highly important and persuasive. The reason is, of course, that this third witness is considered an unprejudiced witness. It is naturally supposed that he is interested only in the facts and not in whether these facts may benefit one or the other party.

The same holds true with anyone trying to persuade another person. If a salesman tells a prospect how good his product is, this is a self-serving statement. Chances are that this will not be as persuasive as or carry the credibility of a story about a disinterested party who used the product and experienced good results.

Facts, Analogies and Comparisons Persuade

No judge will permit opinion, evidence, or conclusions of law by a witness to be entered into the court record.

The same principle holds true with someone you are trying to persuade. Don't think for a moment that he is carried away by your opinion or conclusions. He may be nice, may even appear to agree with you. But you have really offered him no persuasive material.

Get into the habit of using facts, analogies and comparisons to establish belief. If you can present these in story form they are even more persuasive. Don't forget that stories are communication's most treasured vehicles; stories have been the key that unlocks the mind ever since the first faint dawn of speech.

Get Into the Act

The persuasive communicator doesn't just confine himself to telling dramatic stories, but he gets into the act himself. He personally dramatizes the situation when the occasion calls for it. This requires a great deal of judgment, but nothing can be more impressive when the time is exactly right.

Because we hear it so often, we are tempted to put very little importance on the principle that actions speak louder than words. But don't forget that communication is not confined to written or spoken words.

The Ten-Minute Sand Glass Technique

I know a person who dramatically used a ten-minute sand glass effectively. The glass was a miniature hour glass.

When this person walked into anyone's office he would place the little glass on the desk with polite urgency and say, "You are a busy man, Mr. Jones, and so am I. When the sand runs to the bottom of the glass ten minutes will have elapsed. When that happens, if you are not convinced that I can help you, I shall leave quietly and politely. Is that fair enough?"

The glass worked like magic for this individual. Unless the other person spoke up immediately with some objection to the interview, the individual would continue, "The sand is running. In order to save time for us both I must show you this without delay."

The person assured me that very seldom was there even a question as to whether the one he was visiting was going to give him the ten minutes. The dramatic manner of going into the interview so intrigued the other person that he immediately agreed.

The Empty Envelope Technique

A salesman of accident insurance in my city gained many valuable interviews by simply sending an empty envelope to a prospect once a week for several weeks. The return address of the salesman was always on the envelope.

After a few weeks when the salesman made his call in person, the prospect was full of curiosity and naturally wanted to find out about the empty envelopes. This gave the salesman a dramatic lead into his presentation.

"Mr. Smith, those envelopes contained just exactly what you would receive each week in case of an accident, provided you do not have the protection I can give you." The salesman then followed this with a long pause.

Some people undoubtedly will say that they do not believe in gimmicks, gadgets and gismos — that this method of playing cloak and dagger or cat and mouse belongs to a by-gone age. If one feels this way, he should certainly not engage in such activities. But I have known very dedicated people who feel that if a prospect needs their product or service, they are justified in using any ethical means to cause him to accept the benefits and protection which they can offer.

How's Your Story Bank Account?

The persuasive communicator knows the power of a story, an example, a "for instance." He has one to meet every question or objection that might be brought up regarding his product or service. He knows that people will always listen to a story where opinion and statements might bore them. The natural curiosity as to how a story may end keeps a person's attention. Furthermore, it is very seldom that a story can lead to an argument. The third-party aspect gives insurance against such a danger.

Don't neglect this greatest of all vehicles of persuasion. Constantly collect stories that illustrate your points. Not only collect them but practice telling them until you can relate them in an interesting and dramatic way. And most important of all, *use* them. Seek occasions to tell them. They will work wonders for you.

FOUR

The Automatic Way to Get What You Want

The classic answer by the professional boxer, when asked the formula for winning, is "Always fight another round."

There is no better advice that can be given to a person who desires to persuade someone or bring someone to his way of thinking or close a sale than "Always ask another question."

Speakers, trainers, consultants and human engineers give lip service to this theory, but actually very few people place the importance on questioning which it deserves. Did it ever occur to you that the more professional a person is the more time he spends asking questions? This is the surest way of arriving at the truth. We have heard it said many times that it is more important to know the right questions than the right answers because if we ask the right questions, we are going to get the right answers.

An Ancient Greek Mind-Probing Technique

Socrates was one of the first great teachers. His greatness as a teacher was based primarily upon the fact that he led people to their conclusions through questions. In fact, the questioning method of teaching today is called Socratic because it is derived from the methods of this great man.

Starting the Two-Way Flow

The reasons for asking questions to assure good communication are almost too numerous to treat in this book. We shall, however, consider a few.

First of all, since true communication is a two-way flow of ideas and thoughts, asking questions is the only way to guarantee that there is a flow in both directions. This is the very basis of all communication. If we ever forget that there must be participation by both the sender and the receiver, by both the communicator and the respondent, then the whole communication process is born dead.

How to Pinpoint the Problem

Recently I accompanied a friend on a search in a quiet area for a small home to be converted into an art studio.

The first real estate agent we called upon seemed very alert and eager to discuss and show property. In fact, before my friend could tell her complete story, the salesman almost bodily dragged us into his car to show us "just exactly what she wanted."

It is true that we were shown a couple of houses that appeared to be a bargain in real estate investment. They were in quiet neighborhoods where sleep would be relatively undisturbed. We were told, without an opportunity to interrupt or explain our problem, that a mortgage over a long period of time could be arranged. In fact, we were given a 30-minute, rapid-fire lesson in financing.

My friend was so irritated that she completely closed her mind to any ideas of acceptance. She was not looking for an investment. She did not plan to sleep in the structure but only use it for a working studio. She was not concerned with any financing plan for she wanted to pay all cash and save interest.

From what my friend had told me earlier, I felt that either one of the properties would have been adequate to meet her needs. However, her attitude had been conditioned to refusal simply by that salesman's efforts to sell before he even considered my friend's problem.

A Technique That Saves Time

Think how different would have been the whole relationship in general and climate of acceptance in particular if the real estate salesman had observed the first great principle of communication.

What do you suppose would have been my friend's reaction if the salesman had made an approach such as this: "Mrs. Smith, in order that I can save you time and serve you better, do you mind if I ask you a few questions?"

Note that the salesman is even prefacing the questions with a question, a polite inquiry as to whether or not he may be permitted to ask questions. This is the ultimate in professional communication.

His questions should naturally have been in regard to purpose of the purchase, location, size, price, method of payment, etc. In my own mind I feel confident that if the salesman had followed the question route that day, he would have made a sale. My friend later bought a house, which, in my opinion, did not fill her need as adequately as either of the two properties shown us by the salesman.

How to Get What You Want Automatically

There is a law in our economic world as strong as the law of gravity itself. Most of the obstacles for those who offer a product or service could be reduced significantly if this law were fully accepted.

The law: If you spend enough time and effort helping other people get what they want, you will automatically get what you want. If you spend enough time and effort solving other people's problems, you will find that your problems are automatically solved or at least reduced to manageable proportions.

If you are offering a product or service, you have to communicate to the other person that your interest is primarily in solving his problem rather than disposing of your product, that your compulsion for service does actually exceed your passion for gain.

Of course, this means starting the interview with a series of questions to clarify and pinpoint the actual problem of that person.

Please never forget that until a person has agreed with you just exactly what his problem is, you are not communicating with that person. You are only talking to yourself, just pounding your own eardrums. I am sure no one would ever consider this to be communication.

A Two-Way Interest

Remember this cardinal principle of two-way communication when offering a service or product: the eagerness of your respondent to listen to your story can never be any greater than the enthusiasm you show in wanting to solve his problem. The depth of his interest in your product or service will depend on your interest in him.

Making the Initial Approach

While it is necessary to believe in your product or serivce, sometimes, if the most important aspect of communication is neglected, this great belief and enthusiasm can be a handicap.

I've known people who were so dedicated and enthusiastic over what they were offering that their initial approach was to communicate all the fine qualities of their product or service rather than first to inquire as to the problems and needs of the prospect.

Regardless of how sincere a person might be and regardless of his belief in his service or product, notwithstanding his loyalty to his company, his whole effort to communicate is of no avail if he forgets this principle.

Measure of Value

People too often neglect a certain principle that is helpful in encouraging us to ask questions.

That principle is this: A bargain is measured only by the extent to which something solves our problem.

Then doesn't it follow as the night the day that we cannot put any value on a product or service until we ask enough questions to determine the value to the other party? Maybe there is a great value and maybe there is no value. In either event, communication is static until we have ascertained this fact.

A hunting lodge has a great value to a man who is an avid hunter. To others I am sure it would only be a liability.

A fine library is a fulfilled dream to one person. To another it's only so many red, green or blue feet of decoration in the living room.

A surgeon could not render service without his operating instruments. To a bricklayer they would only be articles of curiosity.

These examples are, of course, exaggerated instances, but we can relate the principle to all our activities.

Sincerity in Communication

One of the ABC's of communication is that people are persuaded more by the depth of our sincerity than by the height of our logic, more by our desire to solve their problem than by the brilliancy of describing our product or service.

How often have you heard the expression, "I'm not too sure about it, but he seems so sold on the idea that I am inclined to go along"?

There is the humorous example of the young man who wrote this letter to his sweetheart:

"My Darling, My Dear:

Never did a Romeo love his Juliet as I love thee. For you I would climb the Pyramids; for you I would descend the dangerous walls of the Grand Canyon. Just for a glimpse of you I'd brave the treacherous waves of the Bay of Fundy. For the touch of your hand I'd swim the Hellespont.

I can hardly live until again I can be in the sunshine of your presence.

As ever, your loving

John

P.S. I don't think I can come over tonight. It looks like rain."

The Technique the Professionals Use

One of the first principles that every sales organization teaches its young salesmen is that people love to buy but don't like to be sold. Furthermore, if a person can master the art of assisting people in buying, that is, in doing what they love to do, he has left the amateur ranks and joined the professionals.

There is no possible way for a person to communicate persuasively until he no longer "sells" people on what he wants but assists them in "buying" what they want and until he has adopted the habit of asking questions to find out what they want.

Questions do not have a separate place in any persuasive communication. They should permeate the entire presentation.

The very first sentence of any presentation should be in the form of a question. Analyze your own presentation and give yourself the professional test. Furthermore the second and the third and in most instances the entire first part of every presentation should be a series of questions.

The Question Approach

In the first place, if you start out your presentation asking me a series of questions, I am convinced from the very beginning that you are interested in my problems. Somehow

I get the feeling that you are "tailor-making" something for my particular needs — that perhaps somewhere down the line there is a solution to my problems. You have given me confidence from the very beginning.

When I go to my doctor what is the first thing that he does? Of course — he asks me questions. Immediately he has established the professional relationship. From the very beginning he has turned on little neon letters: *I am trying to find out your problem so I can help you.*

After he has asked sufficient questions and shown his interest in my problem by examining me, I am prepared to accept any reasonable solution he suggests. If he prescribes penicillin, I shall take penicillin. If he suggests rest and diet, I shall change my eating and sleeping habits. If he tells me he is putting me in the hospital for an operation, I simply will prepare myself for the event.

Now why do I buy his recommendations so completely? It is that he has been professional long enough to convince me that his sole purpose is to solve my problem. However, without questions he could never have taken this professional approach and never would he have won my confidence.

A Simple Test

Please, regardless of what may be your line of endeavor in this life, form the habit, in all of your human relations, of asking questions. You will lift communication to the very highest level.

The more professional a person is the more important to him is the process of questioning others. It is said that a doctor spends 80 per cent of his time asking questions and only 20 per cent of his time prescribing treatment. I believe this to be true in all of our sincere efforts to help people.

Give yourself the test: how much of *your* time do you spend trying to ascertain the needs of others and how much time do you spend trying to gain acceptance of your product and service or yourself?

What do you suppose my attitude would be if my doctor spent 80 per cent of his time prescribing a remedy and 20 per cent of his time studying my problem? I am sure I would say to myself, "I hope he is not pushing penicillin this week. I hope the pharmaceutical houses are not giving a trip to the doctor who can sell the greatest quantity of their product. I hope he is not in the last week of a contest to dispose of the largest amount of a certain drug, and needs just one more operation to meet his quota."

The Greatest Compliment

We are all finally accepting the principle today that the word *profession* has a new connotation.

Years ago it applied to a doctor, a lawyer, a professor and a few other areas of endeavor. Today the word "Pro" applies more to the quality than to the type of performance.

I heard someone in a speech not long ago say, "Any society that would scorn excellence in plumbing because plumbing might be considered a humble activity and that would, at the same time, tolerate mediocrity in philosophy because philosophy might be considered an exalted activity — that society never will have good plumbing nor good philosophy. Neither its pipes nor its theories will ever hold water."

One of the greatest compliments we can give to a person today is to say that he is certainly professional in all that he does. This can never be said about a person who offers a product or service unless that person follows the communication pattern of probing into people's problems through the question approach.

What You Have Vs. What You Want

Reduced to the lowest common denominator and stripped to the essence of simplicity, a problem is nothing more than the difference between what a person *has* and what he *wants*. Think about this for a moment. Can you think of any better illustration or definition?

Now this brings us to another consideration: if a problem is only the difference between what a person *has* and what he *wants,* then the extent of a person's problem is simply the distance between these two conditions.

So doesn't it stand to reason that the first two things that a professional problem solver is concerned with are, first, what a person has and what he wants; second, how far apart are these two conditions?

Most people could revolutionize their endeavors if they would only form the habit of finding out these two things before ever considering an offer of their services or product. How completely different would be the entire climate of the communication.

Defining the Problem

Often a person needs assistance in defining and clarifying his own problem. Many times a person calls upon another and finds that he must act in a dual capacity. First, he must help his prospect clarify his needs, and only secondarily, help satisfy these needs.

That is why people who sell furniture, drapes and the like often offer interior decorating services free of charge. Even our large utility companies offer engineering services to their prospective industrial, commercial and even domestic customers.

Bring this principle to your own endeavors. First, ask questions to determine needs. If your respondent is not sure of his needs, by all means proceed no further until, with your help, the needs are clearly agreed upon. Remember, as stated earlier, "Until the other person has definitely agreed with you concerning his exact needs you are not communicating with him, you are only talking to yourself."

Statement Vs. Admission

Which lays a better foundation or creates a finer climate for acceptance of your services or product: a statement by you or an admission by your respondent?

The answer is too simple to need elaboration. I repeat that if you make a statement regarding your service or product, regardless of how true or how brilliant it may be, it is still labeled in the communication vernacular as a self-serving statement. It is not persuasive. It is assumed to be a biased opinion because, if accepted, it benefits you.

This type of communication is given uncomplimentary names such as "hard sell" or "pressure approach."

But let's look at the other side of the picture. The most acceptable and highest form of evidence in law is called *admission against interest,* which means a statement that is ungarnished by prejudice in the witness' favor. This same principle applies in every day persuasion.

If your respondent makes a statement which identifies his problem, then you have already at least one-half convinced him. There is an admission of the need; the problem is out on the table.

Again we return to the method of gaining this admission — the *how* of good communication. It lies in generously asking questions.

I urge you to write the title of this chapter indelibly in your mind. Make it the directional compass of good communication — *Always ask another question.*

Controlling the Situation with Silent Command

We have heard it said many times that a skillful communicator directs the conversation. This is very true but often people are confused in thinking that this means they should dominate the situation.

Well-meaning but misguided communication consultants often urge an individual to keep a higher eye level than that of his prospect. They urge him to speak just a little louder than his prospect. They insist that he take the assumptive attitude at all times.

Always remember that a person's home or office is his castle and that he must be treated as king at all times. Too many people in an effort to be assumptuous actually become offensively presumptuous. This is one of the most basic secrets of Secret Command.

Forget the higher eye level. Don't try to shout your prospect down. You are playing with fire. Not only are such tactics inflammatory — they are explosive!

The best rudder to guide a conversation is the rudder of questions. If you constantly practice this, you will find that results are startling.

Shades of Difference in Communication

Questions offer the very best instrument for testing a person's disposition to accept your ideas, services or products.

In seeking to conclude a transaction, most people are fearful that they will "blow the deal" by moving too fast.

Only the skillful use of questions can prevent such a possibility.

If my respondent's reactions have been so positive that I am sure he is ready to accept my proposal, I would feel safe in such a final question as this:

> From what you have said and based on our conclusions, Mr. Smith, I am sure you are ready to go along on this recommendation right now, aren't you?

This is a bold question, but I don't feel that I am taking a chance because of my respondent's acceptance frame of mind.

However, let's suppose my respondent is interested but has not given me any good acceptance "signals." I would feel safe with a less bold question.

> Mr. Smith, from the information you have given me, I am confident that this is something you should consider seriously, isn't it?

Even though my respondent is not yet fully ready to accept my offer he would want to consider the advantages anyway. Let's take a step even further. My respondent is only slightly warm to the proposition I am offering. I want to be sure that my question is less challenging in its consequence.

> Mr. Smith, if you were sure that this service had helped others in your line of business, you would want to know about it, wouldn't you?

Here you are only getting the decision of the other person to open his mind so that he can consider your proposition.

Questions of this nature should be designed to get a *yes* reaction. Fortunately most questions are so flexible and elastic that they can be designed to receive a positive response from almost any attitude the other person might have.

Consider the last example. Would it be likely that a good businessman would not want the information which his competitors have? Would he take the attitude that even if others were helped by such services, he prefers to remain in the dark and not even know of the benefits? I am sure the situation is very obvious.

Getting Time to Think

While the benefits of questions are legion to a good communicator, don't forget that often a person is caught in a situation where he needs a few seconds to think, to organize a new approach. Many times you can "buy the time" by asking a question.

You may feel that a good listener should concentrate on listening and not be thinking of what he is to say next. As a general rule you are absolutely right. However, there are exceptions to the rule. Often an entirely new thought is brought into the conversation. Many times you will be caught by surprise. This may call for quick thinking or a new approach. A question often will give you this "life-saver." Don't overlook this possibility.

Again I urge you to write the theme of this chapter indelibly in your mind; make it the directional compass of persuasive communication. Remember — *Always ask another question!*

FIVE

The Psychic Compass That Reveals What Others Desire

How to Discover What Others Think

Chapter Four was devoted to the importance of asking questions. Unless, however, we listen to answers the questioning is of no importance. The very purpose of a question obviously is to elicit an answer, to find out a person's wants and needs.

Once we have received an expression of such, isn't it a waste of time and effort if we do not take advantage of the information by listening?

Studies made at the University of Minnesota show that the typical salesman spends 70 per cent of his working hours in communication. This is certainly not surprising because the average person today, in practically every line of endeavor, spends more than half of his time engaged in this activity.

The Minnesota study further showed that this communication activity breaks down into these proportions: nine per cent in writing, 16 per cent in reading, 30 per cent in talking, and 45 per cent in listening.

The amazing conclusion so apparent is that while most of a salesman's time is spent communicating, and although the greater part of communication consists of listening, despite this fact, little time is spent by him in training to be a good listener.

The Inaudible Sound

A friend of mine who teaches physics once told me something which at the time was difficult for me to believe.

He explained that if a dead tree fell in the forest and that if no person was within hearing distance, no sound was made by the falling tree. This of course is correct because it is based on the theory that sound is the reverberation of certain disturbance waves on eardrums. Thus, if no eardrums are within proximity of hearing distance, there can be no sound because the reverberation waves are dissipated into the air.

There is a parallel with communication. When one does not use the eardrums, even though he is in listening distance, there is no communication. While there technically might be a sound, the sound is not audible unless we are listening.

Creative Listening

There is a great difference between passive listening and active listening — between mere tolerance and definite interest. Unless our respondent is actively and energetically engaged in listening, we are not talking to him; we are only pounding our own eardrums. Of course this is a complete waste of time. No one has ever found a way to receive benefits from talking to one's self.

The Psychic Compass

An expert in the field of communication realizes that objections are the best guide to a person's thinking. He receives them as a directional compass that points out the path he should follow.

If we want to be certain that we do not leave any hidden objections the first part of our interview should be designed, with certain provocative statements, to cause the respondent to reveal his thinking. Usually a person gives us this revelation in the form of an objection.

When the objection comes the curtain is raised and the act begins. All has been prologue up to this moment.

At this point it is important for the communicator to listen carefully in order to receive full benefit from the objection. An objection is a signal to listen carefully — not a signal immediately to oppose the respondent's point of view.

Improving the Communication Climate

We all know that objections thrive on opposition but die on agreement.

How often have you heard a person say, "That's just not true, and I can prove it"?

Even if he proves that a person who voices an objection is wrong, he is in a worse position than if he had not. In any event there occurs an immediate breakdown in communication.

How much better it would have been to have been a good listener and heard him out.

Wouldn't the whole climate of communication have been better if he had said: "I am sure you have a good reason for feeling that way. I'd like to listen to you further."

Regardless of how strong a person may feel about something or how emotionally aroused he may be, if we encourage him to talk by indicating that we shall be a good listener, he gradually will let off steam and at the same time give us an indication of his thinking.

How to Get the Cue

If we can divorce ourselves from emotion, and listen as a doctor listens to our heart and lungs in a spirit of diagnosis, often we get the cue which may lead to effective persuasion even in the face of obstacles.

Regardless of what may be your business or profession try the experiment of being a good listener. Let's consider an illustration.

For instance, a supplier might hear from a purchasing agent: "Yes, I'll tell you why we stopped buying from your company. Your company unloaded a bunch of junk on us."

Now naturally the supplier's first impulse is to fight back, to defend his company in the same emotional tone. But remember that in communication we are often faced with this decision: do we want to give way to our immediate feelings or do we want to arrive at our goal?

Isn't it better to assume the role of a good listener? Suppose you were the supplier, and said, "Mr. Smith, I can certainly understand how upset you must have been. Do you mind telling me what happened?"

Now Mr. Smith has the opportunity to blow off steam. Also, while doing so, if you are a good listener, you might find your cue which might lead to correcting the whole situation.

After Mr. Smith's temper has dropped and after he has had his say, you might even hear him say, "In most cases I'll admit that you have given us a quality product but you certainly didn't in this case."

You now have a cue, one you would not have had if you had not encouraged Mr. Smith to talk, then listened sympathetically and let Mr. Smith know that you were truly concerned. He is now more than likely ready to listen to you with an open mind.

How to Follow Through on the Cue

"Mr. Smith, I am glad to hear you say that in most cases we have given you a quality product. This has certainly been our purpose in every instance, and I am distressed to find that in one instance we failed you. "I am sure that in your business you, too, are distressed whenever you find that you have failed in serving one of your customers. Please tell me how we can rectify the situation."

Now at this point shut up and be a good listener. Let him answer you fully. Encourage him to keep talking. The longer you can get him to talk now the better will be your position. He is telling you how the relationship can be glued back again. The more he talks the more he is committing himself to the former relationship. The suggestions are his and if followed he will co-operate. He has saved face. The ideas are his.

Problem Solving Through Listening

While there are many definitions of a problem, perhaps the best I have ever heard and the one we repeat over and over in this book is that it is the difference between what a person *wants* and what he's *got*. Furthermore, again we say that the extent of a person's problem is the distance between what he wants and what he already has.

Now wouldn't it be colossal insanity to tackle a problem before we actually know what the problem is and to what extent it exists?

Unless a person is a good listener he will never know this. The initial step in solving any problem is, through skillful questioning, to get the respondent to express his wants and also tell you what his present situation is. Again I say, however, that this is impossible unless we are good listeners.

Don't Be an Impulsive Respondent

Often a person's maturity is measured by the time which elapses between his stimulus and response.

If a person accosts me suddenly and criticizes some personal action of mine or takes issue with an opinion I have expressed, my first impulse is immediately to fight back.

How much more effective would be my results if I chose rather to be a patient listener and avoid an explosive response. After hesitating a few seconds what if I had said, "Mr. Jones, I am sure that you have given this matter careful consideration and I would appreciate it if you would enlighten me on your views."

A sincere response of this nature is a compliment to anyone. Even if Mr. Jones has a chip on his shoulder, he is inclined to make a mental bow and in so doing the chip will automatically fall off.

Again I say that the more I can encourage Mr. Jones to talk the more intent I should be in my listening. His emotions will inevitably subside. Finally he will not want to be outdone by my interest and politeness, and he will be ready to listen to my side of the story in a fair and open frame of mind.

Good Listening Pays Dividends

Sometimes through careful listening you will receive a gem of information that can pay off handsomely in dividends. Be sure, however, that this will never happen to you unless you are concentrating on what the communicator has to say. Sometimes you will find this through just a word or phrase.

John Thomas called on a wholesaler to sell typewriters. He received the same objection that other salesmen were getting: business was off and conditions were in a down swing.

But John was a careful listener. He remembered the statement by the purchasing agent, "Things would be different if the milis opened again."

When John read in the paper that the mills were opening, he was in the purchasing agent's office within hours and received a large order.

All of John's competitors had received virtually the same story, but John listened carefully and had made a mental note of what other salesmen had ignored.

Why People Don't Listen

Naturally we ask ourselves this question, "If listening is so very important to communication in general and to persuasion in particular, why is it that people resist listening?"

First, it is that so many people are suffering from the

disease most commonly known as laziness. To be a good listener is hard work — it takes real effort. Consequently, most people try to avoid it. They resist brainwork as earnestly as they resist manual labor.

Secondly, only a few people truly realize its importance. Most people erroneously think that they can better serve their own interests by pretending to listen while they are spending their time thinking about what they will say next. Actually, by not listening they have immediately become a party to fractured communication. The channels of mutual understanding have been closed.

And finally, many of us do not listen because we permit our emotions to enter the picture. Emotions cause an immediate hazard to understanding, a barrier to comprehension.

Emotions work in two different directions when it comes to listening. In some instances they can make us antagonistic to the speaker's position. Just as often they can make us over enthusiastic about his presentation.

Whenever emotions enter the picture, we must exercise self-discipline and avoid forming an opinion or making a decision until we can more intelligently and more calmly consider the facts.

How Can We Improve Our Listening Techniques?

The very first principle of improving our listening skill is to school ourselves in the habit of taking time actually to listen. Most of us have the mistaken idea that we are communicating only when we are talking. What could be more erroneous?

Most good persuasive communicators feel that the first part of any good interview should be designed, through provocative questioning, to cause the respondent to start talking. Then it is important for him to realize that he has entered the most important part of good communication — creative listening.

Certainly you must do a certain amount of talking in order to guide the conversation, but by all means remember this.

If the other person interrupts you, immediately stop talking and both politely and energetically begin to listen. If you don't you can be assured that anything you say will be falling on deaf ears. Your respondent is only interested in what he is waiting to say when you stop talking.

How Long Should You Wait Before Answering?

Even when the other person asks you a question, don't be too quick to answer. Don't be impulsive in your response. Regardless of how eager you may be to give an answer, if you hesitate slightly, you indicate that you are considering the question carefully and that you are anxious to use clear thinking and sound judgment.

Also, by waiting a couple of seconds or more before starting to answer, you are insuring that the respondent has finished his question.

Getting Complete Attention

The person speaking wants and has a right to expect more than just casual attention. He wants you to give complete and active attention to his question or position. It is very easy for a person through observing your expression and conduct to determine to what extent you are truly listening. If your mind is wandering, if you are bored or even if your attention is divided, this will be revealed by your manner. You cannot hide it.

Form the habit of giving your full attention. Not only do this but form the habit of letting the other person know through your gestures and expression that you are paying him the compliment of using your maximum listening powers.

Improving Your Concentration Span

The average person's concentration span is short. It is cut even shorter when there are distractions around him.

When listening, try not to notice things around your speaker that will prevent you from a full concentration on what is being said.

The Empathetic Listening Technique

Henry Ford once said, "If there is any one secret of success, it lies in the ability to get the other person's point of view and see things from his angle as well as your own."

When listening, try not to think of yourself as being across the desk or table from the speaker. Mentally go to his side and put your arm around him. Mentally make an effort to put yourself in his shoes. See the situation through his eyes. This is good listening.

How to Use the Psychic Compass to Help You

Regardless of how deeply and sincerely you believe in the art of creative listening, unless you adopt the principles contained in this chapter and in fact form the habit of using them, your roots will remain in sterile soil.

Take these principles and relate them to your particular business or profession. Commit as many as possible to memory. Form the habit of reviewing them periodically. Put them into practice. Make them your listening habits. Like a "psychic compass," they will point the way to Silent Command of others.

SIX

The Secret of Kinesics

That form of non-verbal communication known as body language has become popular here in America almost overnight. It is known as *kinesics*.

While this is hailed by many as a new and exciting science, actually it is the oldest form of communication known to man. Long before man learned to talk, his primary means of making his thoughts, demands, threats and fears known was through body communication. He has never given up this form of expression over the many centuries. He has only added other methods of communication to supplement it.

Even a casual reading of portions of the Old Testament gives examples of this body communication. Is there any doubt in anyone's mind what emotion Moses was showing or what message he was conveying when he threw down and broke the tablets at Mount Sinai after finding his people worshiping the golden calf?

The pages of history are full of examples of body communication.

Triumph or Surrender

Even during early civilizations certain body actions became symbolic of messages to be conveyed.

Kneeling or lying prostrate was a symbol of surrender or recognition of authority. The subject always knelt before the king or ruler. Even the vanquished armies would lie down in acknowledgment of surrender. Later the symbol became raised hands over the head. This was to show that there were no concealed weapons.

Victory in early days was accompanied by a triumphant entry into the city, with the victors riding horses or in chariots. The conquered walked on foot in front, or followed behind in chains. Our modern parade today is an outgrowth of this triumphant entry.

Later when new weapons were used, the surrender of the sword and the laying down of arms became the new symbol of surrender.

Hidden Meanings in Kinesics

Does it ever occur to us to wonder why a man who accompanies a lady down the sidewalk, walks on the street side keeping her next to the building? This is a symbol of protection.

In years past practically all streets were muddy and had pockets of water. Naturally the horses and carriages would splash this mud and water up on the sidewalk. By putting himself between the lady and the street a man was protecting the woman from the splashes of water and mud.

In walking down an aisle at church or elsewhere or in escorting a lady at a party the man has his escort on his left arm. This custom had its origin during the period when a man wore a sword for protection. By having his lady fair to his left, his right arm was free to reach for his sword as protection at a moment's notice.

Another interpretation is a little sentimental and one to which I personally would readily subscribe. A man's heart is on his left side. It is a display of chivalry and affection to carry a lady next to his heart. The Lord did not take a bone from Adam's foot in creating Eve so that she would be beneath him. He did not take a bone from his head so that she would be above him. He took a rib from Adam's left side so that her place would always be next to his heart

— and that is where man should keep her even in escorting her.

I once heard a very fine speech by a person who was not in harmony with the women's liberation movement. He felt that women would lose, if successful, more than they would gain. He titled his speech *Women's Lib or Adam's Rib*. I shall not take sides in this book, but I must say that this person presented a very moving argument in behalf of the theory that when God made Eve from Adam's rib he intended for her to remain at Adam's side, next to his heart and under his protection.

Is There a Founder of Kinesics?

Many people ask who was the first person to do an exhaustive study in the field of kinesics. Certainly no one in this century can make this claim.

One of the first was a Frenchman named Andrew Delsarte, who lived in the early part of the 19th century. He was a teacher of music and drama.

In 1892 one of Delsarte's former students wrote a book on the Delsarte system and entitled it *Gestures and Attitudes*.

Today's Kinesics

Not long ago when lecturing to one of my classes on the subject of kinesics, I asked the students to write on the board as many non-verbal body communications as possible which are used today.

Starting with such simple symbols as saluting, tipping one's hat, opening a door for another, pulling back a chair, shaking hands, throwing a kiss, waving good-by, bowing one's head, pointing one's finger, covering one's eyes, bowing from the waist, puckering up for a kiss, shaking a fist, stamping a foot, winking an eye, smiling, frowning, showing one's teeth and hunching one's shoulders, over 100 were written on the board in less than 20 minutes.

Kinesics Reveals Local Customs

I was invited to dinner while speaking in a Southern state. My host was the program chairman of the meeting I addressed.

He and his wife had five children. As we sat down for dinner each held the hand of the person next to him or her as they said the blessing. I, of course, entered into the ritual which impressed me very much.

When I said what a beautiful thing this was, the host told me that this had been a custom in his family for many generations. He said that this spoke the language of thankfulness for their family circle. This was an impressive example of kinesics.

One of the youngsters assured me, however, that it had another purpose also. He said that this gave every member of the family an even break when hands were released to reach for the biscuits.

Body Contact

One form of kinesics can be either very effective or inflammatory or even explosive. That is body touch.

If it arises from a natural feeling and if it is genuine and sincere, it can carry a great message — far more effectively than words.

An older man may put his hand on the shoulder of a boy or young man as he counsels with him or gives him advice. A boy may gently take the hand of a girl as he pleads his affection for her. A person may take the arm of an elderly lady in a protective manner.

However, there is a sanctity of individuality and a barrier of privacy that no one has the right to invade in others. Unless there is a close intimacy between two people, not only should one not take the arm, hold the elbow or touch the other person, but he should maintain a respectful distance.

Often when I conclude a speech a number of people are nice enough to file by, shake my hand and thank me. Nothing pleases a speaker more. However, there are usually one or two people who want to stand for five minutes and tell me some old story or give me an example I can use in a speech or relate to me the long story of their lives. This is a calculated risk that every speaker must encounter.

In practically every case the person will hold your arm or sleeve in a gesture that communicates "You cannot get away until my story is finished." The moment a person grabs my arm I can identify him as one of those compulsive touchers. I've checked with other speakers and every one of them relates that he is assaulted by these people who can't resist the bodily contact.

Kinesics Is an Honest Revelation

Since our body language usually is stimulated by our sub-conscious it is usually more reliable than verbal communication. In fact, many times it contradicts what we say verbally. Since our subconscious is honest in the things it does, it is well to observe closely the actions of others regardless of what may be the words.

Those who deal in criminology claim that kinesics, if understood properly, is the best lie detector of all. If the body language and the verbal language are completely out of harmony, one can rest assured, according to the criminologist, that the person is hiding something. Later in this book we shall elaborate on the meaning of certain body language.

What Pupil Widening Means

A speaker at a food convention recently gave a report on a study which impressed me very much. He explained that in food chain stores there is never enough display space for items of food that the store owners want to offer. Consequently there is always great competition by food suppliers in wanting their particular brand to be given preference.

It is now a known and accepted fact that the pupils of a person's eyes enlarge, sometimes to twice their normal size, when the appearance of something delights them.

This speaker said that stores are installing hidden moving picture cameras with telescopic lenses that will record the dilation and contraction of the buyer's pupils as he or she looks at the packages on display. The lens is carefully concealed so that the buyer is not conscious of being filmed. The reaction must be under normal conditions.

This pupil reaction, according to the speaker, is far more reliable than any verbal survey that can be made from door to door or from verbal interviews at the store.

Painting the Face from the Inside

Expressions on others' faces convince us far more than words. If a person told me how happy he was and how much he enjoyed my company while he frowned and curled his lips in a snarling and sarcastic manner, I assure you I would not believe his words. By the same token if you smiled at me tenderly and gently with a sparkle of admiration in your eyes while telling me that you disliked me, I am afraid I would be neither offended nor convinced.

Now let's go a step further. All of us agree that we paint our faces from the inside. Our appearance is primarily the accumulation over the years of our past thoughts, impulses, desires, disappointments and emotions. Our present facial appearance and expression is the best recorded history of our past. Lincoln said that every person after 40 is responsible for his own looks.

Then doesn't it stand to reason that often our facial appearance is far more reliable than anything we can tell a person about ourselves? Why not form the habit of being observant in this regard and actually place real importance on character study which involves facial appearance and expression?

Pantomiming

The greatest of all comedians have been those who excelled in body communication. Perhaps Charlie Chaplin was the first of the greats in silent films. Buster Keaton, Ben Turpin, Laurel and Hardy all depended upon nonverbal entertainment for their popularity. Jimmy Durante and Red Skelton are equally great today.

If I were asked to pick the greatest single piece of acting, I would certainly consider among the first a pantomime skit of Red Skelton imitating the old patriotic soldier watching a parade go by. No verbal rendition could ever approximate the revelation of emotions which was accomplished through body communication. The last scene of the old soldier, hardly able to walk, following the parade on his cane, was enough to bring tears to the eyes of everyone.

Entire Scene in Body Communication

Just before the comedian Bert Lahr passed away I had occasion to see him perform.

He went through an entire 20-minute scene with Nancy Walker, and neither spoke a word. The audience was in a state of frenzied hilarity throughout.

As I recall the pantomiming, it was as follows: Lahr, dressed in a construction helmet and heavy shoes, walks in carrying a lunch pail. He slams the door angrily but Nancy ignores him. He slams it again, still gaining no attention.

He angrily opens his lunch pail, takes out a large sandwich with one bite out of it. Lahr glares at Nancy, takes the sandwich over and throws it in the garbage pail, takes a seat in a chair and begins reading the paper.

Nancy goes to the garbage can and gets the sandwich out. She gets a knife, cuts off the piece of sandwich with the bite out of it, wraps the rest of the sandwich in wax paper and puts it back in the lunch pail.

Similar non-verbal scenes continued for the entire time

It was almost unbelievable that an audience could be kept in convulsions for 20 minutes without a word spoken.

Masked Faces

Most people, fully realizing that they reveal their thoughts and feelings through their expressions, make an effort at times to hide their thoughts and feelings with a blank appearance. Did you ever ride the subway in New York City and look at the expressions on people's faces? On most public conveyances in large cities people wear a masked expression to hide what they are afraid they might otherwise reveal.

This practice is part of the protective armor of our society. We want to keep our inner lives to ourselves and at least not share this with strangers. In some countries of the East women actually wear real veils, not just imaginary ones, in order to hide their emotions from other people. Decency requires this.

One of the hardest things for some people to do is to remove this imaginary mask, relax and actually be themselves. They are in reality afraid to be natural. They do not realize that people are most attractive when they are themselves. If a person can't be attractive being himself, he certainly can't be acceptable trying to be something which he is not. People only exaggerate their faults and accentuate their shortcomings when they try to be something that they are not.

Like an Old Shoe

One of the nicest and most complimentary things that can be said about a person is that "he is like an old shoe." What is meant is that he is comfortable and relaxing to be with. We don't have to be on parade around him. He accepts the best in us and ignores the worst.

Above all else, we know that he is not wearing a mask. We accept him for what he is, and we don't feel that we must wear a mask either because we know that he accepts us in like spirit.

A person who does not reveal his thoughts and emotions around us by his expression causes us to clam up as a protective measure. Did you ever analyze your own reactions when you meet up with a "frozen-faced" person? You are immediately on guard. You find that you, too, retreat behind a mask.

A Costume Party

Did you ever wonder why a costume party generates so much gaiety and enthusiasm? It is because people know that their thoughts, feelings and emotions are not on parade. They can let their guard down. No longer do they feel inhibited. Since they are wearing a mask and hiding their emotions or since their costume diverts attention from their normal physical appearance, they have a feeling of escape from inspection.

The advice is so often given to "try being yourself." People who show an appearance of artificiality cause us to withdraw mentally and emotionally.

Dropping the Mask

People who under ordinary circumstances wear an imaginary mask will often, during times of tragedy or other unusual events, drop the mask and reveal their true feelings through non-verbal communication. Think back over your lifetime and ask yourself if at some time you have not been witness to just such an experience.

Many years ago I was taking a trip as part of a "packaged tour." About 30 people were on the tour. On the first day people only glanced at each other in a suspicious or curious fashion. No one wanted to make the first approach for fear that he would be refused and have his ego damaged. The same cold atmosphere prevailed that night. I was sure that we all were destined for a cold and impersonal four days.

During the middle of the second morning we had a blow-out, a thing which seldom happens to a bus. Everyone got off the bus. We were stranded out in the middle of nowhere. Unfortunately the jack would not function. Although cars stopped, an ordinary jack was not sufficient.

For four hours we waited for delivery of a message requesting a jack to be delivered and for the jack to reach us.

During this time people began to realize that they all had something in common; they all were hungry and stranded in the desert. They became very communicative. They took their masks off.

A little ranch house a half-mile away in the desert was sighted by one person. He went over, asked the owner to sell him a few groceries, then made several sandwiches which he brought back, along with some ice-cold pop.

By the time help finally arrived the entire group was hilariously laughing at their own plight. They talked freely, joked, and had completely dropped their guard. No one would believe such a transformation could come over a crowd in just a few hours.

The four-day trip turned out to be highly interesting and enjoyable to everyone. I am sure that friendships were started which perhaps last even to this day. All masks had been dropped and people communicated freely, non-verbally as well as otherwise.

Why Remove the Mask?

Some people might ask why they should drop the mask and let their non-verbal expression be communicated to others. They may feel that they have a right to privacy.

While it is true that we all want a certain amount of inviolable privacy at all times, it is a dangerous situation if we protect this privacy too far. No one is an island unto himself.

In the first place an exaggerated privacy stunts our emotional growth. We cannot learn to develop any meaningful relationships with others.

I once had two very dear friends, a husband and wife. Both were very brilliant people in the scholastic world. Each had a Ph.D. The wife had written a very fine book. The man was highly successful on the speaking circuit.

After about five years of separation back and forth, they finally were divorced. While both were attractive people and intelligent in many ways, neither was warm or expressive facially or in any other non-verbal means. Each, when speaking to me about the other, used the same expression, "I feel locked out and I don't seem to be able to break through."

Sometimes in our effort to protect the sanctity of individuality, we prevent an exquisite intimacy, without which no marriage can be totally successful. There is such a small shade of difference between privacy and loneliness. I've known people who finally take one step outside of themselves and arrive at happiness.

Sometimes it takes an unselfishness which a person does not have in order to drop the mask. One prefers the retreat to one's own privacy above the joy and companionship and affection of friendships and even marriage. Try a study of yourself. Don't be deprived of the great adventure of this world in an effort to preserve a so-called individuality which some people falsely feel they should keep by remaining locked up in a shell.

Table Positions and Silent Command

While we shall, in another chapter of this book, elaborate on the meaning of certain physical gestures, I would like to suggest that you start observing the position which people are inclined to take at a table. This is most revealing of the place in society which each person feels he occupies.

From time immemorial the leader of any group has always sat at the head of the table. We find this to be true whether he be king of his nation, leader of his group, or chief of his tribe. The place of authority is at the head. By sitting there, he is in Silent Command of the group.

This custom still exists today. At a banquet we honor

people by seating them at the head table. It is a courteous gesture; it is a non-verbal communication. We are in fact telling these people that they are important and that we want to give them the V.I.P. treatment.

The family position of authority has historically always gone to the father. That is why we always find him at the table's head. In rare instances we find the mother there. You can be sure that in such a case she has assumed the authoritative role in that family.

Not only does the chairman of the board of a company occupy the authoritative seat at the table, but usually those who are next highest in authority are closest to him in the order of their importance.

Kinesics of a Round Table

Since many nations are jealous of their prerogatives and will not take a secondary position at the conference table with other nations, the only way that some nations will sit together is at a round table. In this way there is no head or foot of the table.

One of the first recorded uses of the round table is found in stories of King Arthur and his knights. King Arthur wanted complete democracy in his court. He didn't want any one knight to be given preference over others. Consequently the custom of the round table was given birth. Those of us who have read literature of that day recall, however, that the plan didn't work too well. There arose great jealousy as to who would sit nearest the king.

Who Picks Up the Tab?

If you are at a dinner club and see a group of people at a table, who do you think will pay the tab? The host in practically every case is at the head of the table — he is in authority there. Everyone else is there only by invitation.

When a man takes his wife or a boy takes his best girl out to dinner, why is the woman seated on the inside of the booth and the man on the outside? It is because he is in the

position of protection, in the authoritative position. He is
the intermediary between the woman and the outside world.
If she needs a second cup of coffee, he orders it for her.
It is he who handles the situation and pays the bill.

Body Communication Speaks Constantly

From the time we wake up in the morning until we go
to bed at night we are communicating constantly by our
body actions — we never cease. We might even go beyond
that and say that we communicate in our sleep.

If I overeat or if I am battling with some mental or
emotional problem, I toss about at night in a very restless
manner. If I have a sound night's sleep, then I am communicating with my body that all is well. I am not disturbed.

Then I think we can safely say that body communication
takes place 24 hours throughout the day and night. It constitutes honest statements because it comes from our subconscious. Consciously a man may lie, but subconsciously
he cannot. Since this type of communication is so important
to us all, let's be a little more conscious of it. Also let's
read this chapter again and study it carefully.

SEVEN

Kinesics and Silent Command

It is said that words are the fingers that mold the mind of man. Others tell us that one picture is worth ten thousand words. Actually all of us realize that the more methods of communication we can put into effect the more articulate we can be. We must learn to be expressive in as many ways as possible.

How to Read People's Minds with Body Language

During many of my seminars on persuasive communication people will ask the age-old question, "Merlyn, how can I be sure of the proper time to cause people to act?" In selling we call it the close.

Please remember this: when we attempt to persuade a person he is usually on his guard. He is very cautious about anything he says for fear he is committing himself. However, he is not cautious about his body language. Because of his efforts to conceal his feelings verbally he is often more articulate in his non-verbal communication than under ordinary circumstances.

This is why it is so important for us to be able to read the language of kinesics just as clearly as we can interpret words.

The Moment of Truth — How to Spot It

Have you ever attempted to persuade a person to commit himself, or give his consent to some line of action, and actually seen a positive decision given even though he didn't speak a word? It happens many times. Unfortunately, however, sometimes we miss the cue.

When to Use Silent Command

The most articulate communication, by a person, that he is no longer undecided but has made up his mind is the gentle stroking of his chin with his thumb and forefinger. Usually this is accompanied by a slight relaxed smile. Any indecision by a person is accompanied by a strain which usually is written on his face. When a decision is made, the tension is released, and usually a slight upward curling of the lips is evident.

When this occurs the period of persuasion is over — now is the time for action. Delay no longer!

I've seen the decision made and expressed definitely by actions and yet the communicator continue in an effort to persuade. I've even seen the communicator continue to the point where he causes the respondent to reverse his decision. A person who continues persuading after the respondent has non-verbally made a decision is similar to a hunter who kills his deer and stands there pumping shot into the dead buck.

A Kinesics Technique Worth $18,000,000.00

At a recent convention in Washington, D.C., I had occasion to meet a very interesting person. She was a 74-year-old real estate saleswoman from Oklahoma.

I asked her what her largest single sale had been. She told me that she celebrated her 73rd birthday with an 18 million dollar sale of oil land. She was one of these rare individuals who enjoy perpetual youth.

When I asked her if she intended to retire some day her answer was, "My blood is just as young as yours, Merlyn. Oh, it might be in an older container. Hardening of the arteries will never cause me to retire. I'll only retire if I get hardening of the attitudes." My guess is that she will never retire.

This very dynamic and very wise woman gave me a suggestion in kinesics which is worth passing on to you. She assured me that on many occasions she had realized a prospect had made up his mind to buy when he took a deep breath and released a big sigh. She said that this sigh of relief was the surest form of non-verbal communication that indecision was over and that the prospect was, ready to take action.

Don't ignore this suggestion. Remember, it comes from a lady who made an 18 million dollar sale because she was sensitive to body communications!

What Folded Arms Mean

We have heard it said many times that folded arms mean, "I do not buy either you or what you sell." When I first started speaking on the circuit, I would often look out over my audience and feel almost panicky when I saw a number of folded arms.

Later on when I began studying kinesics I realized that it is the manner of folding one's arms that indicates resentment and signifies that "I am locking you out."

Remember this: If a person's arms are folded firmly and high upon his chest, this is a gesture of refusal. If he leans forward while in such a position it indicates even stronger resentment. If he goes further and has a frown or scowl on his face, the combination even might indicate to some degree an attitude of belligerence.

If a person folds his arms gently and loosely across the lower part of his body, this signifies relaxation and a good mood. Add to this a smile and you have your respondent or member of your audience in a jovial mood.

He Wouldn't Ask Me

I had occasion to talk with a salesman who was very up-set and discouraged because a customer did not buy his product. Since I knew both of them well, I asked the customer why he did not buy.

The customer assured me that the salesman needed some sales instruction. He said, "I always buy from that company. However, this new salesman never gave me a chance. He kept talking and never presented me with the order to sign."

I delved into the matter further and asked the salesman what the objection had been. He told me that the customer had folded his arms and locked him out when he first sat down. He explained to me that it would have been useless even to try a close under such circumstances.

If one is to play the kinesics game, one must be an expert at it. Here was a salesman who had lost a sale because he misinterpreted body communication.

The King's Protector

We have all noted pictures of the palace guard or the king's protector. He is always the big person standing erect with folded arms and a stern expression on his face.

This communication has carried over into today's customs. Note the person who stands guard at a hotel's private party or one whose assignment is to see that some dignitary or celebrity is not accosted by the public. Invariably he will carry himself in a manner to discourage any trespass. His body language says, "You are locked out; don't try to enter."

What Eyes Reveal

Above all else get the habit of watching the eyes of people you are seeking to persuade.

If a person looks you straight in the eye in a pleasant manner without trying to stare you down, you can rest assured that this person is interested and perhaps will give you a fair consideration.

However, if the person is shifty-eyed and refuses to look at you directly, or if he drops his eyes — beware! This person will also be shifty in his verbal communication. Don't rely too strongly on what he says to you.

I've had occasion to see many respondents look up at the ceiling or cast their glance upward and rapidly blink their eyelids. This is a clear sign that they are considering your proposition seriously. In most cases this communicates the fact that they have already decided in your favor on the big issue. They are merely considering the details such as when, where, and how many. If you doubt this at all, study such a situation the next time it happens and you will find that among the dozen or more common methods of body communication this is one of the most reliable. Very seldom does it fail.

Raising one's eyebrow indicates disbelief while raising both eyebrows shows surprise. Winking one eye can be flirtatious, or if the person is too far away to communicate verbally, it can mean "I agree with you 100 per cent," especially if the wink is accompanied by a slight nod of the head and a smile.

Don't Ignore Shoulders

The use of one's shoulders is a very articulate and vivid form of body communication and yet very few people take time to consider this.

A person who "hunches" his shoulders or raises them casually communicates indifference. If this is accompanied by the raising of the eyebrows and even curling of the lips downward it communicates very strong indifference. He is definitely saying, "I couldn't care less."

A person who carries his shoulders in bent-forward or "hunched" position does not give us the impression of energy or determination. Don't always rely on this, however If there is some physical defect that forces this posture, our diagnosis could be completely wrong.

It is particularly distasteful to see a young person in a slouched position. We immediately feel that we are in the presence of a person who has no ambition, who is not an organized person.

What Posture Tells You

By contrast, a person who stands erect with his shoulders upright radiates determination and energy. Merely by throwing his shoulders back and holding his head high he is communicating to us, "I love what I am doing, I know where I am going, and I intend to get there."

Did you ever wonder why a military school puts such great emphasis on correct posture with the shoulders thrown back? In fact, this is the first thing that is emphasized to new students. The reason is very simple. Authority, courage and determination are three things that must be learned if a man is to become a good soldier. Good posture radiates all three.

How would you feel if you saw a battalion of soldiers go by all bent over with their shoulders humped? Would you consider them a victorious group? Would they inspire confidence, or give you a feeling that you were protected? Our armed forces are concerned with building an image, a proud image. We even speak of the "military carriage" of one's person.

How to Feel More Confident

There are many reasons why a person should communicate confidence and ambition by good posture. Of no little importance is the fact that it has a great effect upon the person himself. Go to the mirror this moment and look at yourself. First hang your head, hunch your shoulders, and say, "I am a forceful individual. I am engineered for accomplishment, designed for success, and endowed with the seeds of greatness. There is absolutely nothing on the face of this earth that I cannot accomplish, if I so desire."

Do you sound very convincing to yourself? Did you buy the idea?

Now go back to that mirror. This time stride up to the mirror confidently with your head high and your shoulders thrown back. Now say the same thing. It makes a difference, doesn't it?

I don't intend to go into the controversial theory as to whether a person laughs because he is happy or is happy because he laughs, but I assure you that you cannot build an image in the eyes of another unless you first carry that same image in your own mind's eye.

How to Listen to Complex Body Language

Recently I took part in a management clinic in Dallas, Texas. After the clinic I was talking with one of the speakers, who told me that he and his family were moving to Denver. My first impression was to congratulate him and tell him that I thought it was a great idea.

Just behind him, however, I noticed that his wife was standing with one foot thrust forward, her head held high, and her chin thrust slightly upward. Her lips were pressed together tightly, her shoulders thrown back, and she had each of her hands on the shoulders of their two children who were very close to her side.

This picture told me much. Fortunately I checked myself before saying anything and passed over his statement with some casual remark.

I was very glad that I had followed this procedure because later that evening the wife told me very definitely that she was not about to take the children out of school and move to Denver. She even indicated that she did not know whether the family would ever move to Denver.

Don't you think you could improve your communication quotient if you formed the habit of "listening" to body language as well as verbal language? Why not try it for a week?

You will suddenly realize that there is a message which you have been ignoring all of your life. Don't use only a fragment of your listening ability. Be a "pro" and master kinesics.

Avoiding Offense

While giving a clinic on kinesics to a real estate firm not long ago, I asked those present to give any outstanding observations they had had in this field. One salesman in particular related a very sad incident, an experience, he assured me, that would never happen again.

This salesman had been showing a large ranch to a prospective buyer. He had spent about three days with the gentleman, who seemed very interested. In fact, the transaction was verbally agreed upon. All was accomplished except working out a few details and having the contract drawn up and executed.

While discussing a minor point, the salesman walked around the desk, put his arm around the gentleman, and patted him on the far shoulder. The gentleman stiffened, reddened, got up and walked out of the office and never came back.

The salesman asked me to analyze the situation for him. Not knowing all the facts and not having had the opportunity to observe the incident I could not be fully helpful. But please, *please* never take the liberty of bodily contact unless you are very sure of your ground. Not only do many people resent this, but they are actually offended and highly insulted by encroachment on their privacy. I emphatically discourage even the use of another's first name until the other person has made the initial approach. If you are a salesman, by all means let your prospect take the first step. Over the long haul you will find out that this is best.

How to Notice the Small Body Whispers

Not all body communications are to be taken too seriously, but it is at least well to be able to interpret them.

For instance, do you ever try to understand the emotion of

a person who rubs his nose while you are making an effort to get a decision from him? In most cases this is an indication of disapproval, disagreement, or even resentment. Of course the energy with which a person does this often tells us a great deal about the extent of his disapproval or resentment. When we observe such conduct it is well for us to consider carefully our next move. We have been told very clearly that the person is definitely not in the frame of mind to O.K. a contract or declare himself in favor of something.

Hands Over Eyes

Can you recall ever having seen a person suddenly throw his hand over his eyes? This, of course indicates that he is ashamed of something. It's a way of non-verbally apologizing to you for some thoughtlessness.

Slapping One's Forehead

You have forgotten something and you want to be demonstrative about it. What do you do to show the other party that you did not remember? Many of us slap our forehead and even close our eyes. This is in reality a combination of showing that we have forgotten and asking for forgiveness.

Fingers Together

If a person holds his hands in front of his chest with the fingers of each hand touching the same fingers of the other hand, it signifies confidence. This person is fortifying his remarks by saying in body language, "I know what I am talking about. I am something of an authority on what I am telling you."

This is a characteristic pose of my doctor. I have observed this on many occasions and I do not resent it at all. In fact, I have now begun to watch for it and am even a little disappointed if he does not do it at least once when I have an appointment.

The next time you have occasion to attend a conference where there are several panelists sitting at a table on the platform, please watch for this non-verbal means of communication. I give you a full guarantee that if you observe carefully you will see an exhibition of this more than once.

Public Kinesics

I once had a contest at a clinic to see who could name the greatest number of well-known statues that were created to give some body communication.

On this occasion there were over 30 such statues named. Among those named were The Thinker, Diana, Cupid, The End of the Trail and numerous others. The Thinker led in number of selections. Give yourself the test. Also note that every city of any size in the United States has one or more such statues. I was in Salt Lake City the other day and had occasion to observe four within five blocks of each other.

Drumming Fingers

Elsewhere in this book the point is stressed that an interview is not a true interview unless we are with a person both physically *and* mentally. Only then does true persuasion begin.

While a communicator may be with his respondent physically, you can be sure that he is not with him mentally if the respondent is drumming his fingers on the desk or table. Please note that in many cases where the respondent is tapping the desk or table with the fingers of one hand, his chin is resting on the other hand. These two gestures go together.

When you find yourself confronted with this situation, don't waste your time proceeding with the interview unless you can capture the person's interest. Any further presentation is like water on a duck's back.

Foot Signals

Many people like to sit in a position where they can observe the action of a person's feet.

If the respondent is moving his foot around nervously in a circle, he is portraying the same impatience that he would show by drumming his fingers.

However, if the shoe hangs loosely on the toe of the foot, this indicates relaxation; in fact it is a very encouraging gesture. Women in particular often are engaged in this gesture.

Change of Position

One of the most important facts to remember in the study of body communication is that change of physical position usually indicates a change of mental attitude. Sometimes this change is in favor of the persuader and sometimes it is against him. In any event, the moment that a person uncrosses his legs and leans forward, or folds his arms and leans back, or puts his hands behind his head and looks up, or makes any other obvious change in physical position, this is a cue that a *mental* shift has just taken place also.

Watch for Body Communication

It is impossible to discuss all of the physical gestures that tell us what the other person is thinking. Space does not permit it in this book.

I shall feel well repaid if I can only convince you of the importance of constantly watching for these gestures. You will be astounded when you realize how quickly you can master the art of interpreting the body language clearly.

Please form the habit of observation in the field of kinesics. When you do form this habit you will find that a new dimension in communication has opened to you.

EIGHT

Space Communication and Territorial Invasion

There is a most interesting phase of non-verbal communication, equally important with body communication, known as *space communication*.

Much is being written about this subject today. It has been given many different names by many people. Some have titled it "Zone Studies," others call it "Spaceology," still others have called it "Territorial Invasion." One even coined the name "Proxemics."

It is unimportant what we call it, but it is very important that we understand it, especially the important part it plays in today's communication.

The Territorial Need

Since the dawn of civilization everything that walks, crawls, flies or swims has had a territorial need. It is not enough to have space to live in. Whether for animal, fowl or fish, there must also be territorial identity.

The lion has always had his area that he dominates. It is clearly marked with boundaries just as definite as those boundaries a farmer might claim for his farm. The wolf pack has its definite run. Even fish and birds have habits of territorial occupancy.

So sacred is living space to people that it has been the basic cause of practically every war ever fought. It has been the moving factor that led to the discovery of new continents.

The settlers moved west because of the desire to acquire new territory.

Law Recognizes Its Sanctity

Man's very sanctity requires him to have geographical identity. We have always heard about the sanctity of the home. This is the one space that man can call his own. So sacred is it that the law recognizes the right of a man to protect it even if it requires the death of another.

Maybe some of you have read the book, *A Man Without a Country*. If so, you were impressed with the fact that a man has a great void in his life if he has no place where he can stand and say, "This is my own, my native land."

Sanctity of Space Transfer

While a home or other real estate can be transferred today merely by the delivery and recording of a deed, it was at one time far more difficult. There were no written deeds and no recordings. The method was as follows:

All of the people in the area were gathered together for an all-day festival. Food, drinks and entertainment were provided. Finally toward the end of the day the preacher gave a prayer. The person transferring the property would take a handful of the soil and hand it to the person receiving the transfer as symbolic of title transfer. Furthermore, the transferor would place his hand on a Bible and swear to defend the transferee's right to the property as long as he lived. Then after a prayer all of the people would walk together to all four corners of the property where the boundaries would be identified in the presence of all.

There was once a rather strange custom connected with a transfer. A boy from the neighborhood was chosen. At each corner of the property the boy was given a sound thrashing. This was to impress upon his memory just where the boundary lines were. If, in later years, there was a boundary dispute the boy so chosen was considered the expert. His testimony carried much weight. Besides the fact that he perhaps would live longer than the older people and be around more years to testify, his memory was thought to be more vivid since he had a good reason to remember each corner.

It was considered a great honor to be the chosen boy for the ceremony. However, I am not sure just how honored the boy himself felt, or whether he volunteered or whether he was given this honor against his will.

Space Encroachment

Everyone of us subconsciously feels a possessory right to a reasonable amount of space near ourselves. If we are sitting in a plane or bus next to someone, it is an unspoken law that each of us has a right to our particular territory which no one can invade.

Even if we are having lunch with an acquaintance this same rule holds true. We subconsciously divide the area of the table equally and are disturbed if there is an encroachment on our area. It is instinctive with us. Many times when an encroachment such as this occurs, we become upset and don't realize the cause of our emotional arousement.

The Spoon Episode

I was invited to speak at a banquet in Sarasota, Florida. At noon on the day of my engagement I was having lunch with the program chairman. After lunch we were talking and having coffee. For some strange reason I was conscious that my luncheon partner had leaned back from the table with his arms crossed indicating a body communication which said he was resentful of something I had said or done.

For a moment I was puzzled. Then I realized that I was playing with my spoon and that I had placed it over on his side of the table. He unconsciously felt an encroachment of his territory — I had invaded his space. After realizing this, in a relaxed manner, trying not to be obvious about it, I pulled the spoon two or three inches back from his territorial line.

The reaction was almost immediate. In less than one minute he was leaning forward in a friendly, relaxed manner, talking with me and smiling. I'm sure this person did not realize, and I of course did not tell him, that he had just been the guinea pig in a space encroachment experiment. I had, in effect, given him the Silent Command to be friendly.

A Fascinating Experiment

There is an old western song that says, "Don't fence me in."

Westerners are noted for their strong territorial consciousness. We see many movies today which have plots built around the fight between the cattlemen and farmers over the fences.

However, everyone of us has a fear of restriction of movement which applies to the foot or two of space that surrounds us.

On the day following the Sarasota incident I had been so intrigued that I made another experiment. I was sitting at the counter in the airport next to a very expressionless man. I gradually eased my knife and fork over close to his territorial area. I then casually sipped water and put the glass down slightly over in his space.

After a few nervous movements this man put his elbow down between us, thus staking his claim, rested his chin on it and pivoted around slightly, putting his back toward me. He obviously was fighting against the encroachment on his territory as strongly as possible without making a scene. I gradually withdrew my attack, but it was too late to get any change in his conduct. He did not trust me any longer. He kept his elbow and back as a defense wall and even ate with his left hand.

My experiment would have been a total success if I could only have been sure that he was right-handed. I wanted to ask him but I was not quite too sure where experimentation ended and aggressiveness began. So I rested my case without further effort.

The Mental Satisfaction of Space

I have a friend who owns a lovely home in the mountains only an hour and a half from Phoenix. She uses it fewer than a half-dozen times a year. She has refused several offers for it at figures which she admits are far beyond its worth. I have asked her on several occasions why she did not sell it. It is obvious that the limited use she makes of it doesn't even justify the expense of taxes and upkeep, much less the investment of money that is tied up.

My friend finally confided in me that the mountain home communicated a certain freedom of choice to her which had become very valuable. She said it meant a lot to her just to know that she could go up to her mountain home any time at the drop of a hat. She did not feel a territorial confinement because she was not limited to her home in Phoenix. I am confident that many people keep a second nome for that reason and do not fully realize it.

The Deepest Human Need

After a speaking engagement in Chicago, an elderly couple came up to me and asked if they could talk with me for a few minutes. I agreed to meet them in the coffee shop within 15 minutes.

This couple first asked me about Arizona in general and then specifically about a certain subdivision of two-and-one-half-acre plots in northern Arizona. I gave them all the information I could but had to confess that I had not heard of the subdivision.

I was amazed when they told me that although they had owned the plot for seven years, they had never seen their land or even been in the state of Arizona.

However, they seemed happy over their purchase. They

assured me that they had already received a twofold return on their money just from the joy of knowing they were not forever confined to the limits of their place in Chicago.

Some day, they assured me, they would retire to their ranchero in Arizona. This was a dream of liberation from a restricted territory.

Psychologists tell us that the deepest human compulsion, next to the law of self-preservation and next to the sex urge, is the desire to own real estate. This compulsion arises from the fact that it is this real estate which gives us the space freedom which man must have.

Please Keep Your Distance

It is a generally accepted fact that the varying distance which we must keep between our body and that of another is determined by the degree of our intimacy. This is not only good taste, but relationships are also conditioned to this principle over a long period of time.

We have occasions to observe this every day. I was at a cocktail party the other day in a rather crowded room. A lady was sitting at a table in the presence of three men. A fourth man came up and sat down very close to her. He immediately patted her on the knee. She looked at him and smiled approvingly.

This was very articulate non-verbal communication. This little drama which took place in three seconds told me a great deal. This man was the husband. He had a right to occupy a space close to this woman. If any other man had sat that close, it would have been an invasion of her privacy, a violation of propriety and conventionality. The placing of his hand on her knee might even have been considered an insult. But a husband and wife enjoy an intimacy which does not extend outside the marital circle.

Mental Halitosis

During the years when I was receptionist, I had occasion to observe good taste and bad taste in the handling of space by people who called at our company.

The most irritating of all callers is the person who on his very first call practically crawls all over your desk trying to be a regular guy. Within minutes he wants to call you by your first name. Not only has he invaded your territorial privacy but your personal privacy as well. People such as this have mental halitosis; they simply brighten up the office when they leave.

The Privacy Zone

The person I liked and admired was the person who always stood a respectful distance away from the desk and politely and in a businesslike manner stated his business. This communicated courtesy and respect. Even though such a salesman and I may have eventually formed a friendship which permitted a first-name salutation, still I always desired to see that the intimacy of my desk zone was not invaded.

By standing at a respectful distance that person was communicating to me, "You are an important person in this company. You are even more important to me because you are the *only* person who can make it possible for me to see my prospect. Your desk is your office. Just as I would not bound into your office without being invited, I shall take no liberties with your desk or the close proximity therewith."

How Distance Communicates Respect

Have you ever been in court and noticed the position of the lawyer as he pleads his case?

Legal etiquette, my lawyer informs me, requires that he stand a full six to eight feet away from the judicial bench. Occasionally the judge may call the two lawyers involved up to the bench and speak to them in a tone of voice which cannot be heard by the jury or witnesses. The lawyer never penetrates the dignity of this zone unless it is by invitation of the judge.

The non-verbal communication on the part of the lawyer is very obvious. He is, by keeping his distance, proclaiming that he has utmost respect for the judicial system of our country and that he is not one to violate its canons.

The Appearance of Intimacy

There is another reason why lawyers are expected to keep a respectful distance from the judicial bench. If a lawyer and judge have been too closely associated in former practice of law or in any other way, that judge is required to disqualify himself in a case wherein that lawyer is involved. There should be no intimacy between the judge and any lawyers appearing before him.

Closeness of physical contact suggests intimacy, whether it be true or not. Therefore, the very appearance of intimacy should be avoided. A lawyer who tries to be too intimate with a judge is immediately suspected of ulterior motives, perhaps even of tampering with justice. For these reasons and for numerous others a lawyer is expected never to invade the judicial zone.

The Big-Top Table

To a lesser extent the chairman of the board and even the president of a corporation often have a large desk which is six or eight feet across. This means that they are protecting a large territory of intimacy. They can keep people at a distance.

This principle can be carried a step further by having an office for the private secretary or assistant through which one must pass before getting to the chairman or president. This extends their territorial control even farther.

A definite problem for many heads of corporations is the need to discourage a junior executive from trying to become too "palsy-walsy." A good chief executive can't even give the appearance of showing favorites. A large desk discourages this. If the junior executive is kept at a respectful distance, it is difficult for him to have anything but a respectful attitude.

Violating Zone Barriers

There is the type of person who, though well-meaning, has the unfortunate habit of letting his nose practically touch yours when he is speaking to you. You feel that this person, however innocent he may be, is invading your territory.

Most animals don't like their privacy invaded any more than man does. You can walk up to within a few feet of an animal at a zoo. If you go too close, he will move away.

There were a couple of little squirrels that would come up to our door at the last home where we lived. We often fed them nuts. About three feet was their territory of intimacy. If we came closer, they ran away.

Don't get the habit of violating zone barriers. It is not only bad manners, bad communication, but also it makes you personally become obnoxious.

NINE

How to Listen with Your Eyes

I once asked a very successful person to name the one quality which he considered most important to his success. Without a moment's hesitation he said, "I try to listen with my eyes as well as with my ears."

Reading Others' Minds

If this chapter accomplishes nothing else, I hope it can encourage you to form the habit of using your eyes to listen. Since we see a hundred times more than we hear, if we form the habit of using our eyes for listening as well as seeing our exposure is increased a hundred fold. Don't forget that listening is just as important as speaking in good communication. So if you can start listening with your eyes, you will start receiving messages which might make other people's minds an open book to you.

Visual Listening Reliable

"I know it is true because I saw it myself."
"Seeing is believing."
"Don't take his word. Go and see for yourself."
"Show me."

How many times have we heard the above expressions? In the spoken word there is a great margin for error and misunderstanding. Maybe the person who delivers the message is uninformed or perhaps he colors the statement through self-interest or prejudice. He might even use words that have one meaning to him but a different meaning to us. Noise interference might cause a complete misunderstanding.

This margin of error is greatly reduced when we draw our conclusions from personal observation.

I recently read an account of a trial in which there was a great variance and conflict of evidence. An accident had occurred on a bridge. No two witnesses described the bridge in the same way. Finally the judge instructed the jury, accompanied by the bailiff, to go out and inspect the bridge. The message given by observation, by *visual communication,* was more reliable than the testimony of all the witnesses.

Verbal Vs. Visual Communication

I heard a person humorously tell a long, wild story involving a personal experience. His wife, taking the story seriously, contradicted him, saying that she was there and the facts were not stated correctly.

The husband chuckled and said, "Another good story ruined by an eye-witness."

While the husband had purposely exaggerated the facts and had related the story with tongue in cheek, there is a good lesson in this story. Do we give to visual communication the credibility which is its due?

Convincing Actions

Have you ever heard the expression, "His actions speak so loudly that I cannot hear what he is saying"? This is just a way of saying that his visual communication is in conflict with his verbal communication since the first is so much more convincing, it drowns out his words.

As a ridiculous example, what would be your reaction to a man who spoke to a temperance organization while highly under the influence of whiskey? Even if the contents of his speech were brilliant, he certainly could not be persuasive. There would be a definite breakdown in communication.

An ardent suitor might proclaim his affections for his sweetheart to the high heavens. He might write her letters every day and compose poetry for her by the page. Soon, however, all of this would lose its persuasive power if he never made a proposal of marriage.

Less Say — More Do

The old slang expression, "Less say — more do," carries an important message. Verbal assurance soon loses its veracity unless it is backed up by action.

Last spring I took part in a five-day seminar, sponsored by a city in Iowa, on "How do we sell our city?" I was very much impressed with the motto of the city, "It's good to live in Keokuk." The whole climate of the week's seminar was built around the usual theme that business goes where it's invited and stays where it is well treated.

None of the city's propaganda, however, impressed me as much as what the citizens, through their Chamber of Commerce, actually did for new business. I am sure this great little city will continue to grow and enjoy new business as long as it continues to communicate through action as well as words.

Use This Tested Technique

All of us are prone to accept important principles mentally and yet fail to use them to our own advantage. Form the habit of better observation, of listening visually. If you concentrate on listening visually, you can soon form good observation habits.

Why Some People Get Hired and Others Don't

On one occasion I was engaged to recruit a number of women to do some survey work for a large national company.

Their job was to call on consumers and obtain reports on their buying habits.

On some occasions I would be aware of certain mental reservations when I employed a person. I could never quite put my finger on the exact reason for my hesitancy. Almost invariably, when I had these doubts the people turned out to be unsatisfactory. During the interview their answers to questions were satisfactory and past records of employment seemed O.K. Then what had prompted me to be skeptical?

On careful analysis I finally concluded that it had been the non-verbal communication which I had received at the time of the interview. Carelessness of dress and grooming on the part of some had been evident. I recalled a sloppiness of posture in one instance. Just the lack of assurance and confidence in the appearance of another had been observed.

Listening with Your Subconscious

I had been so anxious to be fair and unprejudiced in my selection of people for the assignment that I had based my selection almost entirely on the answers I received from the questionnaire and from their past record of employment which they themselves had submitted.

Our subconscious mind is not influenced by emotion and is not blinded by unimportant details. Furthermore, it bases its decision on credible evidence, visual observance being one of the most important. The subconscious is the best listening device we have. I am confident that none of us rely on its good judgment as we should.

Your "Sixth Sense" and How to Use It

Many of us vaguely refer to a sixth sense which we might possibly possess. Sometimes people are almost afraid to refer to this except in humor. If a businessman reported to his superiors that he had made an important decision based on this sixth sense, all eyebrows would be lifted.

Actually our sixth sense is one of the most, if not *the* most powerful and reliable mechanism for judgment and decision-making which we possess. It is our God-given subconscious mind. Through our subconscious alone can we comprehend reliably, uninfluenced by extraneous matters. Our subconscious knows no favorites. Its judgment cannot be warped by flattery, fear or undue influence

How to Turn On Your Magic Communicator

Did you ever hear a person say, "I'd like to sleep on it. If I feel the same tomorrow as I do today about it, I shall go along on the idea"?

Now what is this person truly saying? Whether he knows it or not, this is what he feels:

"My subconscious is more reliable than my conscious. You may have influenced me unduly. I am not sure. Perhaps I have other things crowding my mind so that I cannot see the picture clearly. In any event I need reassurance. This comes to me only when I feel securely about it as well as think securely about it. I am putting this proposition completely in the hands of my subconscious mind. My subconscious is the supreme court in all my decisions. When I go to sleep my emotions will subside, my worries will cease, and I will not be subject to influence from unrelated matters. Tomorrow you will have your decision — a definite decision — and one that I shall have the courage to back up with action."

Please don't fail to avail yourself of this "Magic Communicator" — your subconscious. It is the most reliable listener you possess. Also, when it speaks to you, you be sure to listen. It is the one oracle which is yours.

20-20 Communication Vision

If you saw a certain fowl in the company of ducks and if it quacked like a duck, had feathers like a duck, and laid duck eggs, you wouldn't have to send for a veterinarian to find out that this was a duck. Just the simple power of observation would communicate that fact to you.

And yet in our everyday experiences we have things communicated just as forcefully to us, and we fail to use our 20-20 communication vision and accept these truths.

Employment Vision

The president of one of our nation's largest automotive industries once told me that the most costly mistake his company makes has to do with errors in employment of the wrong people for the wrong jobs. When I asked him the cause of these mistakes, he said without hesitation that it was because those who have the responsibility of employment too often take into consideration facts which should not be considered.

When I pressed him even further for information, this man of great experience said that in his considered judgment there were only two factors which should be given major importance in employment:

First, *the past record of the applicant.* The president assured me that the pattern of a man's conduct in the past is the best information on which to predict his future. People fight against change. Any change in their environment or in their conduct makes them feel insecure. Never can we find a more reliable prediction of a man's future conduct than his past record.

Second, *what is he doing now to prepare himself for greater opportunities in the future?* The president was very emphatic about this second criterion. He said that one should not take into consideration what the applicant plans to do about preparation in the future, and should not even give a great deal of consideration to courses he has taken in the too-distant past. The real test is what he is engaged in at present that will improve his capacity to do a better job.

How to Impress an Interviewer

One might wonder what communication has to do with employment.

When a person applies for a job, we can be sure that he wants to communicate the best impression possible. Consequently, we can be sure that all verbal communication is colored with personal interest. It would be very strange if it were any other way.

This is why an employer must resort to facts in order to make the best appraisement and best prediction of the applicant. An applicant naturally will want to impress the interviewer with his sincerity and his desire to do a good job. While this is all fine it cannot compare in importance with the sincerity and desire which the applicant showed in the past.

Body Language Is a Two-Way Street

We all hear the statement, which I repeat, that "Communication is a dance and it takes two to tango." This is just as true in body communication as in verbal communication. For instance, when I first started speaking on the circuit I concentrated intensely on the body language which I spoke to my audience. I practiced before a full-length mirror day after day and week after week. It was several years before I realized that the body language spoken by an *audience* to a *speaker* is just as important.

So let's take a look at non-verbal communication first by a speaker and then by an audience.

The Casual Friendly Approach

Unless my audience knows more about their particular business or profession than I, they have no right to attend the convention where I speak. And so the stiff, scholarly approach, as though I were a philosopher with a basket of sage knowledge, ready to hand out intellectual calories to all who can digest them, is out. Also, the use of gimmicks, gadgets and gismos is usually corny and leaves an audience cold. Even if one can keep complete attention, it doesn't mean that he is successful in his mission.

People attend a convention to get helpful information. If I can present this information in an entertaining way so that it can be remembered, then the audience will not have attended my session in vain.

If I want to be sure that I can accomplish this, I must have my subject matter so completely under control that I can think intensely while appearing physically to be relaxed. I must communicate the idea that I have a very important message to communicate, and that both the audience and I are going to have fun while I reveal this message.

This is why I always like a "roving mike" where possible. If I can move about and even walk among the members of the audience I can increase the informality and create a relaxed climate which I feel is important in my case.

Getting Attention with Gimmicks

Just as slang is an excuse and a poor substitute for good English, I feel very strongly that a speaker who uses an excessive number of gimmicks is offering a poor excuse for good body communication. While it is true that gimmicks can get attention, what a speaker really wants is favorable attention, attention to himself so that he can convey a helpful message. He can bring on the dancing girls, explode a firecracker, or have a bunny crawl out of the birthday cake, and eye-catching and surprising as these may be, they cannot capture the attention which can be created with good body communication.

Three Miracles of Body Communication

To be sure that he brings about the desired results, in a good convention presentation a speaker attempts to do three things. Body communication plays an important part in all three.

First, the speaker should see that the whole climate of his presentation is relaxed and informal. His facial expression, gestures, strolling among his audience and movements in

general are far more important in this respect than anything he has to say.

Second, since an audience wants not to be talked at but
rather communicated with, participation is vital. Frankly,
I have oratorical claustrophobia. I cannot stand planted
behind a podium. I want to cruise among my audience, ask
questions, and get complete involvement. Lately I have
added a new feature to this involvement. I call it "participation reward." Those who are attentive and participate are
given little prizes. Sometimes it is a record of one of my
speeches, sometimes just a 25 cent item, but this reward
keeps interest high.

Finally, don't take yourself seriously — concentrate on
your audience and your subject matter. I've seen speakers
who could be great platform artists if they could only learn
to take one step outside of themselves, look around at themselves and laugh.

If a speaker lays an egg, which every speaker will do sooner
or later, he should call his audience's attention to it and then
ask them to laugh with him at it.

Recently I was taking part in a seminar in Regina, Canada.
A speaker who preceded me got his tongue twisted three
consecutive times on a rather difficult word. I was embarrassed for him and I could feel the embarrassment of his
audience.

However, this speaker smiled, took his glasses off and
began cleaning them as he said, "I spent a thousand dollars
having my eyes fixed and now my mouth won't work."

His audience went wild with applause. Not only did he
break the tension but he made his audience love him. Any
time a speaker can exhibit a sense of humor at his own
expense, he is certain to win his audience.

Any speaker who can do these three things — create a
climate of informality, gain participation, and emphasize
the importance of his audience — will always be in demand.
However, he can never accomplish all this without a generous
use of body communication.

The minute I see more than two people in my audience
looking at their watches, staring into space, or folding their

arms high upon their chests, I know that one of two conditions prevails. Either my time is up and I should close, or
I must make a quick change of pace by getting immediate
participation or taking some steps to capture my audience's
attention.

The Invisible Barometer

Salesmen have an expression; when one sells a product to
a customer, then talks so much the customer changes his
mind, the salesman is said to "buy back his product." The
tragedy of tragedies in speech making is when a speaker
makes a good speech, then "buys himself back" by continuing to speak when he should shut up.

I make a point of picking out two or three people in my
audience who were the last to give me their attention.
These are the most important people to me. They constitute
my "invisible barometer." I watch them closely throughout
my speech. Usually they will be the first to become restless.
I then want to close my speech or change the pace before
the other, more patient members of my audience become
restless.

How to Take Calculated Risks

In many audiences a speaker has one or two people who
only "came for the ride," who just wanted to be with the
other people. They are bored with themselves and everyone
else. They not only pay no attention but they also communicate to the speaker that they can hardly wait for the
speaking ordeal to end. In this respect they are usually
very articulate.

This is the calculated risk of being a speaker. Nothing
can be done about it. While it annoys and distracts a new
speaker, one must learn to live with such a situation.

The only procedure for a speaker is to ignore them and
cling to the people who seem interested. As Mr. H. B. Swope

once said, "I cannot tell you the formula for success, but I can tell you the formula for failure: try to please everyone."

I might add that in some instances I have, when getting my audiences involved, corrected this situation by choosing an uninterested and bored person to do some role playing in front of the audience. It is rather amazing how many times such a person turns into a complete "ham" and seems to enjoy the limelight. My conscience usually hurts me when I resort to this, however, because participation should be a reward for attention. Most of the people actually love to be chosen for role playing before the group.

We have touched on just a few non-verbal forms of communication that have to do with listening, employment, platform speaking and dealing with people in general. Please read this chapter again and relate some of the principles found herein to your own experiences. Don't confine your understanding and participation in the great field of communication to mere writing and speaking. There are new horizons to observe and new worlds to conquer when we become experts in body and other non-verbal means of communication.

TEN

How to Project
Unspoken Orders That
Must Be Obeyed

A body of information given by someone to another person or to a group is a *presentation*. There will always be two philosophies of thinking on the subject of whether or not a presentation should be "canned."

One group insists the presentation should be completely prepared, that a straight line is the shortest distance between two points, and that this straight line can be followed only through a well-prepared presentation, followed meticulously.

The other group takes the stand that the completely prepared presentation is amateurish and unprofessional in every respect. They claim that any parrot-like presentation does not take into account unexpected events that might take place in the course of any interview.

Your Psychic Road Map

While I do not intend to champion either of these two theories totally, I am sure we all agree that communication in all facets and in all fields is far more effective if we follow certain basic patterns of procedure. For instance, I would not start out driving from Los Angeles to New York without a road map. Just to head out in an eastward direction would be colossal insanity.

Regardless of how correct the road map might be, however, and notwithstanding how carefully I might have studied it, I could not follow it blindly. Maybe a bridge would be washed out, or a detour sign might appear. A highway department might close a mountain road due to a snow storm.

Secret of Structured Thinking

Then doesn't the intelligent approach seem to be something of a compromise between the two theories? Whether we make a speech, present a product or service, ask for a raise, hold a meeting or engage in any other form of important communication, we must have an outline of procedure or formula to follow. I like to think of this outline or formula as the steel girders of a building being constructed.

Regardless of whether we finish the building in brick, cement, glass or marble, this steel structure is necessary. If the color of the building be green, blue or black, still the basic frame must be there. If it be equipped with elevators, escalators or stairs, the steel structures must be there to support any of these.

How to Move People to Action

While it is true that much communication is designed only to educate or entertain, the real purpose of most of our communication in dealing with people every day is to cause them to act.

During this century there have appeared many different patterns of persuasion. All of them are effective when properly followed, and all are designed in their ultimate purpose to cause people to be moved to action.

Basic Formula for Action

Perhaps the first of the different formulae for persuading people to act became popular around the turn of the century.

It is found in all instructional books published by insurance companies and many other companies for their salesmen. It contains the three basic elements — pose the problem, offer the solution and ask for action.

The Crasher Technique

Just after the depression of 1929 a number of personal development schools sprung up everywhere. People were discouraged and were reaching for something. Out of these, the Dale Carnegie schools survived and became popular. They have been an important factor in sales and personal development over many years.

We find four elements in their pattern of persuasion. These were "Ho-Hum," "Why Bring That Up?", "For Instance" and "So What?"

In the Dale Carnegie classes a student was often given the assignment of standing before the class and presenting a speech. As the speaker faced his audience, the other students would say "Ho-hum" and indicate how completely bored they were at that moment and how unconcerned they were over anything they felt the speaker might have to say. This was a challenge to the speaker to open with a "ho-hum crasher" and get their attention. This might be done with a question, a provocative statement, or even by flashing an exhibit.

Then the audience would chant in unison, "Why bring that up?" It was now important for the speaker to explain to the audience why the subject brought up was important to their welfare — why they should listen.

Then the students would say, "For instance." This was a cue for the speaker to give an illustration or tell a story to prove his point.

Finally the audience would say together, "So what?" Now the speaker must tell the audience what he wanted them to do about it. He must appeal for action.

The Dale Carnegie formula is not limited to speaking or selling. It applies to every line of endeavor. This pattern reminds us that there is no excuse for effort except for action — no reason for action except for results.

Basic Selling Technique

Still later another formula took its place in most of our sales training sessions and development programs. We called it the "Attention, Interest, Desire and Action," or A.I.D.A., procedure.

The Third Dimension Technique

As human engineering becomes more popular, we have still another approach. It is sometimes spoken of as the third dimension approach.

The advocates of this theory maintain that while "what people do" and "why they do it" are important, these are important only to the extent that they can guide us in the most important phase of dealing with people, namely "how to cause them to do it." This theory is in reality an outgrowth of the "Attention, Interest, Desire and Action" pattern. It simply tells how one accomplishes the fourth facet of that program.

We must get a person's *attention*. How? By making him *like* us.

We must get his *interest*. How? By making him *understand* us.

We must get his *desire*. How? By making him *believe* us.

We finally must get *action*. How? By making him *trust* us.

So we can see in this pattern of persuasion the words *attention, interest, desire* and *action* have been replaced by the third dimensional human engineering words: he must *like* me; he must *understand* me; he must *believe* me; he must *trust* me.

Selecting the Right Method

I am confident that if a person went out and used any of these patterns enough and used them sincerely, he would be successful. But one of the great things about freedom of speech is that we have the blessings of choice.

Do yourself the favor of selecting any one of these or any

combination of these that will make you comfortable in your communication.

The Cundiff 4-Ply System

Over the years I have both taught and lived all of the above patterns of communication and have finally ended up with that which serves my purpose best. I feel comfortable with it. It is in harmony with all of the above but slightly different from them, because it uses "Silent Command" techniques, as well as the conventional ones.

I'd like to give it to you and elaborate on each part. The four steps which I suggest are these: present the problem, offer the solution, prove my case, and then ask for action.

The First Step

It is very important that in your initial effort to communicate in a way designed eventually to lead people to action, you must take the four steps in their logical sequence. Once you present any one of them out of proper order, the pattern will become chaotic.

The biggest mistake most of us make is that in our eagerness and enthusiasm to offer a solution and persuade other people to act as we desire, we fail to put due emphasis on the first step. This first step is the very essence of my whole formula. Unless you have a problem to solve, a need to fulfill, you have nothing to perform. It is similar to an effort to come back from a place you have never been.

How to Make Others See Things Your Way

You must agree with your respondent about the problem. Bear in mind that by "respondent" I may mean one other person, a group, or even a whole audience. In every case, that other person, group, or audience, must see the problem as you see it. It is not enough if you fully explain to the respondent just what you think his problem is. He must agree and commit himself to recognize the problem.

In fact, your first step is a sale within a sale. Until your respondent has bought the idea that he has a problem, and put himself on record that he has a problem and knows just what it is, you have no reason to consider going on to your next step.

As I have said earlier, a problem reduced to its simplest terms is nothing more than the difference between what a person has and what he wants. Sometimes your respondent needs your help in establishing these two conditions. Usually the first condition does not offer any great difficulty, but the second condition is much harder to establish.

In any event, don't let your enthusiasm for what you are proposing cause you to neglect this first step. Remember, pin it down definitely. Get the other person's unequivocal commitment on this point.

The Cloak and Dagger Technique

Many feel that you should not even approach this first step until your respondent's attention is fully gained. They favor gimmicks and gadgets to attract this attention even before discussing the problem.

I firmly believe that unless the problem can be presented and discussed so forcefully that in itself it receives complete attention and interest, we shall fail in this first step anyway. Be careful about playing cloak and dagger or cat and mouse in an effort to get another's attention. This is not the way to get favorable attention.

If attention were all I needed, I could burst into a person's office or home in a rude and insulting manner and get his attention every time. I might even get some quick action. But what I want is *favorable* attention.

Now let's suppose you have discussed your respondent's problem fully and that he has agreed with you just what it is. You are now ready for the next step.

The Second Step

Unless your proposal offers a solution to your respondent's problem, you have no excuse for even taking up his time. Your very presence there would constitute mental dishonesty.

In initially offering the solution, your manner must carry the enthusiasm which springs from your own conviction. Unless you are so sure your proposal satisfies his needs, unless you are positive that you have already solved his problem in your own mind, you cannot expect him to buy the idea.

The Subjective Sale Technique

In emphasizing this point at salesmen's seminars I always try to stress the "subjective sale." Unless the salesman himself completely buys the idea that he has the solution to the problem, he will never sell his prospect. Yes, this is the *important* sale. Fortify yourself with this conviction — arm yourself with sincerity. You are then prepared to discuss the fact that you have the solution to someone else's problem.

The Third Step

It is not enough merely to tell your prospect that you have the solution to his problem. Necessary as it is, even a deep conviction on your part that you can help him is not sufficient.

You must offer proof — convincing proof — that your proposal is his answer. This is done in many ways. You should always be prepared to offer plenty of evidence in this regard. Remember that mere statements and your opinions are self-serving and do not carry a great deal of weight. Offer quotes, give "for instance's," tell stories of other people's experiences and the happy results which resulted.

How to Offer Proof That Convinces

If you ever sat on a jury, you will recall that the judge in his instructions to you carefully told you that in considering evidence you must put more importance on facts, events and happenings than on mere statements by either party which might be to either's benefit.

I repeat that since time began stories and "for instance's" have been the greatest of all vehicles for persuasion. Everyone can relate himself to a story. Stories are understandable — they convince.

I again emphasize even more strongly that the most moving of all arguments is the fact that others "did it and are glad." Stories and for-instance's are our best method in this regard.

The "Q" Technique

Don't forget to use quotes where possible. The value of this type of persuasion is evidenced by the many, many testimonials we find in our national advertising today. Just the fact that some well-known athlete or other celebrity did something has a big impact. So valuable is this in causing people to accept a product or service that large fees are paid today for testimonials. I call this the "Q" technique.

The Fourth Step

Let's suppose that you have been successful in getting your respondent to agree on just exactly what his problem is. He listened carefully when you presented your proposal as a solution, fortified your position by giving an abundance of proof that your idea had solved many other similar problems for other people. This brings you to the fourth step. In fact, the first three steps are important only to the extent that they prepare your respondent for this fourth step. Yes, unless we get action the whole interview is merely a waste of time on everyone's part. But, by now, you have already planted your "unspoken orders" in his mind, so you're all set.

How to Ask for Action

It is almost unbelievable how many people are excellent in the art of persuasion until they get down to the point of causing the other person to act. Here they fail. If these people could only adopt the philosophy from the very beginning that there is no excuse for effort except to bring about action and no excuse for action except to bring about favorable results, they would be far more successful in good persuasion.

Refusal Is Not Rejection

All of us have a great compulsion to guard our own ego. One of the deepest human impulses is the desire to be accepted, to be a part of something. By contrast, when we are neglected or rejected we are hurt. The opposite of love is not hate, it is neglect and rejection.

Perhaps the principle reason that so many people are afraid to ask for action is that they fear the emotional trauma of being rejected. This puts our ego into a nose-dive. Since all of us are trying so hard to protect this ego, we have difficulty pursuing this fourth step just as strongly and sincerely as we handled the first three steps.

About the third time the average person receives a refusal of his proposal or idea, he accepts this refusal as a rejection of himself. This is something which a person must overcome if he ever expects to be professional in the art of persuasion. I have a friend, a great human engineer, who told me that whenever he gets a refusal he tells himself that what this person is really saying is, "I like you very much, but up to this point you have not given me enough evidence to cause me to act. Please see if there is not something else you can tell me which might persuade me."

Don't Fear Fear

I have never been one who subscribed to the feeling that one of our great freedoms should be freedom from fear. Fear is normal; it is part of nature's law of self-preservation; it is inoculation against laziness and complacency. However, fear can never lick us if we are not afraid of fear. Naturally we dislike refusals but let's never be afraid of them.

Many people mistakenly think that courage is freedom from fear. This is not true. Courage is proceeding in spite of fear. It is certainly no disgrace to be afraid. However, it is inexcusable to let fear overcome us.

The Built-In Vince Lombardi

Many stories have been circulated about the great Vince Lombardi. I heard one in particular just before he passed away which impressed me very much.

A first-year player had been working his heart out in practice for hours. Vince said to him, "Go into the showers. You're about the lousiest football player I ever had on the field."

About an hour later when the team went into the dressing room, there the rookie was crying like a baby. He was too tired and broken up even to take off his shoulder pads.

Vince went up to him, ruffled up his hair and said, "Son, I meant it when I said you were a lousy player. But I want you to listen carefully while I tell you something. I mean it. Someday you are going to be the greatest tackle the Green Bay Packers ever had. And the reason is that you are willing to work and, furthermore, I shall always be right here to guide you and encourage you and see that you are."

Immediately the kid brightened up and became a new person. He was ready to go out and practice another three hours.

Now the thing that impresses me most about that story is this: wouldn't it be wonderful if everyone of us who becomes discouraged could have a little built-in Vince Lombardi to pump us back up so we are ready to go right back out and exert the second effort?

The number of refusals we get is not as important as our reaction to them and our next step after receiving the refusals.

How to Overcome Objections Quickly

It is perfectly natural that a person who desires strongly to convince another will have, to some extent, an emotional trauma upon receiving a refusal. Yes, it will take a toll on him. He can be likened to a tire that gradually "goes down" as the refusals mount up. But his concern should be in formulating a method to pump himself back up to counteract the results of the refusals.

Throughout this book we suggest time and again the importance of tape recordings, books, records, clinics, seminars, schools and all methods of both increasing our knowledge and being motivated. Don't fail to take advantage of the opportunity.

The Only Action That Counts

Before leaving this fourth step in the art of persuasion, let's accept one principle absolutely: Action is not action at all unless it is *immediate action*. Persuasion takes place in one dimension of time and in only one. That is, of course, *now!*

Too many people buy the statement of a reluctant listener that he will give his consent in the future. Not only does this lead to a waste of time but the person seeking to convince is living in a world of *make-believe*.

A person is so far better off if he will be mentally honest with himself and accept the true fact, hard as it may be, that any decision to act which does not also carry the decision to act *now* is in reality a refusal. What else could it be?

Build your whole approach for action upon a request for immediate action. Stress the urgency of *now*.

Mr. Jones, if you could convince yourself that this will bring you the same profits that it has brought others, you would have no objection to okaying the contract so that we can get this program started now, would you?

Step-by-Step Control Plan

In taking the four important steps discussed in this chapter, let's be sure that we have good rapport at all times with our prospects.

Again I repeat that we must be orderly and completely organized as we proceed from one step to the next.

Physical Interview

It is obvious to us all that until we can get into the physical presence of a person our persuasion does not even begin. Of course we have telephone interviews, but that is not the point of discussion at this time. While I do not wish to dwell on the method of prospecting to secure a physical interview, I do want to suggest just two points to keep in mind:

First, always ask for the interview with polite urgency. It is the immediacy of the interview — the necessity of *now* — which is most convincing. A person always has time for anything which he considers important to him. If you can stress the importance of listening to you immediately, you are emphasizing the most important approach. Let your general conduct radiate this feeling of urgency. Unless you yourself communicate this feeling of importance, you certainly cannot expect the other person to consider the interview important.

Second, never, *never* try to sell anything but the appointment in your initial effort to gain this physical interview. Don't suggest anything except the importance of listening to what you have to say. If you refrain from letting the merits of your proposal become the subject of discussion at the time of seeking the appointment, you will find that the other person has very little or no reason for refusing the interview.

While a person may give other reasons for not wanting to

grant an interview, actually the real reason usually is that he feels that by granting an interview he is, in some measure, committing himself to accept your proposal or idea, or to buy your product or service. We can often dispel this fear with a preliminary remark such as this, "Mr. Jones, you may or may not have need for this. We can quickly find out. However, I feel that it is very important for you to have this information."

Again let me urge you never to attempt anything on the initial approach other than an acceptance of the physical interview.

Mental Interview

Many people have the mistaken idea that just because they are in the physical presence of a person they in reality have a true interview. I've seen a person sitting three feet away from another physically, yet he was ten thousand miles away mentally.

Have you ever seen an individual drum his fingers on his desk, squirm in his chair, and look up toward the ceiling in a manner which communicated the feeling "I wish I knew how to get rid of this joker"?

Please remember that you do not have an actual interview until you are in both the physical and the mental presence of a person. Do yourself a favor: don't take up another's time by even attempting the first three steps of persuasion unless the respondent gives you a mental as well as a physical interview.

Of course you would never be rude or insulting, but if you are convinced that the other party is not willing to give you the attention and interest which your call deserves, just politely excuse yourself with some such remark as, "Maybe some other time, Mr. Smith, when you are not so busy," or, "I am sorry Mr. Jones, I have information which is important to you, but I can see that this is not the time to present it to you." If you are polite and sincere in such remarks, often the whole climate of the interview will change immediately. If it doesn't, you have saved much wasted time for everyone.

Yes, until you are both physically and mentally in the presence of a person, you are not in a position to proceed with the steps in persuasion, namely, posing the problem, offering the solution, proving your case and asking for action.

Emotional Interview

In 85 per cent of the cases where a person is convinced and the decision made final it is while the prospect is emotionally aroused. It is part of human nature that people are moved to action only after they have been motivated. Consequently, everything we have said or done up to the point of emotional stimulus is mere prologue. This is by far the most important act in the drama we call persuasion.

Since people are different, that vehicle which arouses a person emotionally cannot be the same with all people. Pride may be the moving factor with some; profit may be the vulnerable spot with others; the responsive note with others might be need, love, or fear.

The responsibility of a good communicator seeking to persuade is to feel the emotional pulse of the other person and find out, through trial, to which of the above he will respond. This requires communication at its very finest.

I hope you will realize how many of the problems of life can be simplified and reduced to manageable proportions if one can only learn the pattern of persuasion. Go through the steps time and time again. Take certain hypothetical cases and practice these steps. You will receive dividends that you cannot afford to miss.

ELEVEN

Preventing Communication Breakdowns

One of the rewarding things about treating the subject of kinesics is that it is so broad it covers everything we say or do. There is very little danger of getting off our subject. It is like the sky itself. We can never get out from under it.

Take Out Insurance on Good Communication

The first three chapters of this book gave the three fundamentals of good communication: simplifying, relating the subject matter to the other person's understanding, and using stories generously to illustrate our point.

In Chapter Four we took out even more insurance against fractured communication. The proper method of asking questions is a real art. It accomplishes many purposes, but above all else it is the best guarantee that the communicator and the respondent are talking and listening about the same thing.

Chapter Five also gives us certain techniques to make sure that there is clarity of understanding at all times. Creative listening by the respondent not only enables him to get a better picture of the communicator's ideas but also encourages the communicator to keep this picture in focus.

Case Study

Years ago the teaching profession realized that one of the best ways to transmit knowledge on any subject to a person was through the case history method. Law schools began giving actual legal cases to even the first-year law students for study. This method was soon followed by the medical schools. Now the engineering schools and practically all specialized courses of study are built around the case method.

This method of teaching has its origin in the firm conviction that no knowledge or method is fully understood until we can apply this knowledge or method to some specific situation. When we can see thoughts and ideas in action, we have a new understanding and a new concept of what it is all about.

Not only are we able to see all parts in relation to the whole but when end results are in sight all steps seem to take on a special meaning.

Showing the Entire Picture

One of the great dangers of the assembly line in our system of modern mass production is that too often employees only see the small picture of their job performance. How much better understanding they would have of their own job if in their minds they could relate their activity to the completed product. Many companies that realize this fact try to give an employee at least a fair understanding of the other activities which combine with his to make the finished product.

One of the old revived Charlie Chaplin movies shows Charlie in an assembly line just tightening bolts as they go by. Long after he left work each day his arms would spasmodically jerk in the motion of turning that wrench. He didn't understand what he was building. All he knew was that he was to tighten those bolts as they went by.

How to Increase Understanding

There are many versions of the person who just puts together ingredients and one who creates end results. You remember, I am sure, the story of the person who walked up to two bricklayers and asked them what they were doing.

The first one said, "I am laying brick and getting a good wage for it — in fact, double for overtime."

When accosted, the second one said, "I am building a beautiful cathedral, one unsurpassed in beauty and one that will last forever."

No one can doubt that the second workman had a better communication and understanding, even with himself, regarding his endeavors.

Diminishing Understanding

As a child we played a game called "Gossip," in which several children would line up in a row and then an equal number in another row facing them. Someone would whisper a similar story into the ear of the two children who headed each line. Then the children would whisper the story into the ear of the child next to them. Finally, when the story reached the end of each line, the last person receiving it would tell the entire group what he heard. Laughter was always provoked by the entirely different story told by the last listener in each line.

Although this was only a child's game played for fun, it is amazing to note that this fractured communication takes place in so many facets of our business world today.

The Colonel's Command

Somewhere in the records of the army there is reported a story of a certain colonel who was an amateur astronomer.

Many years ago, it is alleged, he gave this order to his executive assistant:

Tomorrow evening at approximately 20 hundred hours Halley's Comet will be visible in this area, an event which occurs only once every 75 years. Have the men fall out in the battalion area in fatigues, and I will explain this rare phenomenon to them. In case of rain, we will not be able to see anything, so assemble the men in the theater and I will show them films of it.

Executive Officer to Company Commander:

By order of the Colonel, tomorrow at 20 hundred hours Halley's Comet will appear above the battalion area. If it rains, fall the men out in fatigues, then march to the theater where the rare phenomenon will take place, something which occurs only once every 75 years.

Company Commander to Lieutenant:

By order of the Colonel in fatigues at 20 hundred hours tomorrow evening, the phenomenal Halley's Comet will appear in the theater. In case of rain, in the battalion area, the Colonel will give another order, something which occurs once every 75 years.

Lieutenant to Sergeant:

Tomorrow at 20 hundred hours, the Colonel will appear in the theater with Halley's Comet, something which happens every 75 years; if it rains, the Colonel will order the comet into the battalion area.

Sergeant to Squad:

When it rains tomorrow at 20 hundred hours, the phenomenal 75-year-old General Halley, accompanied by the Colonel, will drive his Comet through the battalion area theater in fatigues.

This is often repeated as a comical story, but actually in our everyday conversation stories are varied just as greatly as they pass from person to person. I once heard a reliable source described as "the person we just met." An informed source is "the guy who told the fellow we just met." An unimpeachable source is "the guy who started the rumor in the first place."

Garnishing the Story

Often people delight in gossip so thoroughly that they almost deliberately hear a story in its mangled state.

A dear little old lady in my home town once slipped while wearing sneakers and broke her wrist. The story of the event traveled over the community and many different versions of the story were heard.

One lady was heard telling another, "It served her right! Anyone who would sneak up on another or slip up trying to overhear something should have an accident like that."

How to Get the Best Support from Others

Again I emphasize the fact that one of the best insurances we can take against breakdown in communication is to make an effort to get the respondent to see the entire picture. Do you think that an artist could make any major contribution to a masterpiece if he were only allowed to paint one fragment of the picture, never being permitted to see the entire work or even being told what it represented? How skillful do you think an assisting surgeon would be if the primary surgeon did not even let him know in advance what was to be the nature of the operation? Even the assisting nurses could not give the best support unless they were part of the team to bring about ultimate results.

Years ago I had a friend who worked in a large law firm in New York City. He often complained to me that a certain senior partner would give him points of law to research, but he never knew anything about the case to which the points of law applied. He assured me that he could have been far more helpful and thorough if the small fragment of law he researched could have been related in his own mind to the whole case.

In spite of the obvious diminished performance revealed by the above illustrations, we continue to see similar examples every day.

An acquaintance of mine works in a large electronics plant in Phoenix. She told me that she "wires a little gadget" over and over each day. She has no idea what purpose is served by this so-called gadget. She further stated that if she only knew what purpose it served she could guard much more carefully against defects in the wiring.

A personnel executive in General Motors stated that every person under his control, as part of his training, was permitted to follow his contribution (whether it be a section of a generator or a wheel) to its ultimate destination, even if a trip to another plant were necessary. He emphasized that this increased understanding on the employee's part paid off handsomely. It widened the scope of communication with that particular employee.

Improving Efficiency

Not only is greater efficiency encouraged by understanding of the ultimate product; morale of the employee is also enhanced. How long do you think you could remain interested in creating a product or performing a service if you were kept in the dark regarding its use or benefit to another? It would remain a "thing-a-ma-bob" or a "gismo" as far as you were concerned.

Just as we cannot impose responsibility upon a person without giving him authority to back up his responsibility, we cannot ask a person to take pride in his work unless he is given an opportunity to observe the fruits of his labor.

How to Add Value

As vital as communication is, just a very small variation in action can often make a huge difference.

There was a certain grammar school which had two candy stores located an equal distance from the school. These two stores sold the same candy at the same price. They each used the same kind of scales to weigh the candy. Yet a strange thing existed. One of the stores was always full of kids spending their allowance or lunch money. The other appeared on the verge of going broke. Someone made a study of the situation and this is what was discovered:

The proprietor of the busy store, upon receiving an order for a certain kind of candy, would put the little weights on his balance scales. At first he would put only a few pieces of candy on the scales — then a few more — and a few more. Each time he added candy the little purchaser would grin with delight. Finally when the sale was complete the youngster eagerly rushed out with his bargain, a happy customer.

Now let me remind you that the other store had the same candy at the same price. Yes, the proprietor even used the same kind of scales. However, his method of communicating the purchase was far different. This proprietor would put a large handful of candy on the scales. He would then start removing one or two pieces of candy at a time. Finally when the right amount was on the scales the proprietor would put it in a bag and hand it to the little disenchanted purchaser who had just gone through the emotional trauma of seeing what he first thought was a bargain dwindle in size.

Although each buyer actually received the same amount of candy, the two proprietors had communicated an entirely different story. One had been adding value; the other had been taking candy away from a child. Many of us, without realizing it, are guilty of a similar breakdown in communications.

Just a Fragment of the Picture

As children we read the story of the four blind men who visited a circus. They decided they wanted to visit the tent where the elephant was kept.

The first blind man went over and felt the side of the elephant and told the other two that an elephant resembled a wall. The second blind man took hold of a leg and said no, the elephant resembled a post. The third grasped the tail, and disagreed, saying the elephant was like a rope. The fourth took hold of the elephant's trunk, and shouted that the elephant was really like a snake. And they all began to quarrel, because each man got just a fragment of what an elephant is really like.

One of the greatest investments a company or a private employer can make is to invest in the understanding and morale of the employees by making sure that each employee not only understands his own work, but also is conscious of how it fits into the overall picture, into the ultimate results. Regardless of the cost, this is the cheapest insurance that can be taken out as a guard against communication breakdowns.

In your own communication with others, particularly when you wish to persuade them to do something, be sure that they see the total picture, the ultimate results of what you want them to do.

TWELVE

The Vital Secret of Silent Command

We have heard it said many times that all of life is nothing more than a crusade from the cradle to the grave in search of importance. In this trip we go through many emotional hungers and satisfactions. First, we want to be liked, then we want to be understood, then we want acceptance, then we crave to belong to something, and finally we want to be put on a pedestal and be recognized and bragged about.

The whole journey is one stimulated by the desire to feel important.

How to Build Up Others

Consequently, if we want to be sure that we keep the channels of communication open, if we want to be sure that people do not build walls of resistance to keep us out, let's learn to make people feel important. This is the vital secret of "Silent Command."

The world is made up of two kinds of conversationalists. We have those people who know how to build up the other person, guiding the conversation into fields of interest that can make an individual feel informed and at ease. Then we have the other group who only know how to talk about things that interest themselves. They ask no questions of the other person. They simply begin telling of events within the realm of their own experiences. One so-called conversation on their part constitutes over-exposure. They do not know how to engage in actual communication.

Convincing Others Without Effort

Let's consider a few ways that you can communicate this feeling of importance to me.

Give me the first opportunity to start a conversation if we should find ourselves in a situation where a conversation may ensue. If you do this and I begin talking, you can be sure that I shall start in a field that interests me. Even if it is on a subject of which you are uninformed, you will be surprised how well the conversation will progress if you only listen and occasionally let me know you are not bored by asking a few questions.

Maybe you find that I do not start a conversation voluntarily. Then why not ask me a few well-chosen questions to determine what my field of endeavor or my hobby is?

Recently I was in London and found myself sitting next to an English college professor at a dinner party. He seemed very reserved and I was almost embarrassed at the lack of communication between us. Every remark I made was answered, not rudely, but with a brisk and brief "no" or "yes."

Finally I made a real effort. I said, "I have had occasion to work with college students in both the United States and in Canada. I would be very interested in knowing if the college students of England are different in any major respect from those to whom I have been exposed. You teach them and I also understand that you have been a guest lecturer in the States. You have had an opportunity to make an excellent comparision. How do you feel about this?"

The professor immediately opened up. I found I had pressed his "hot button." After we discussed that subject, he volunteered other fields of interest and almost passionately gave a full expression of his views in each case.

At the end of the evening he assured me that he had never met a more enjoyable conversationlist or one more thoroughly versed on so many subjects. Actually, I hardly had an opportunity to say anything and never once had I brought up a new subject. I had only listened enthusiastically and occasionally had asked him to elaborate a little more in detail.

I assure you I was not making an effort to manipulate this person. I was truly interested in the subject I suggested. Through being put at ease in his own field of thought, he felt a sense of importance and became a fountain-head of conversation for the evening.

The Cruelest Thing to Do

One of the cruelest things we can do in the field of human relations is to deprive another person of the right of discovery.

Did you ever have a person tell you the ending of a suspense picture you planned to see? Did anyone ever ruin the reading of a "Who done it" for you by telling you it wasn't the butler or the maid but a person you least expected?

The most lasting lessons of life are those where we are permitted a certain degree of independence in our research and where we finally realize certain truths through our own unassisted discovery.

My chemistry teacher was not only a good science teacher but also a great human engineer. He always kept the excitement of possible discovery before us. This gave us a feeling of importance and an eagerness to pursue our studies. Think how lacking he would have been in his communication if he had removed the incentive of discovery by telling us in advance what results we would find by mixing certain elements or compounds together.

Discovery Applies to All Fields

It has been my privilege over the years to do a considerable amount of training in the real estate profession — especially in the specific field of persuasive communication.

I remember very vividly spending an afternoon with a salesman who was holding open house in a subdivision on the outskirts of Scottsdale, Arizona. A man and his wife were being shown through the house. In an excited tone of voice the lady, as she entered the living room, said to her husband, "Look, dear, the window frames Camelback Mountain. Isn't that fantastic?"

The salesman could have said, "Yes, that's what we have had in the ad all week. All houses in this subdivision are built so that Camelback Mountain can easily be seen from the living room window."

How deflating this would have been and how unkind to deprive the lady of feeling the importance of discovery.

The salesman was a good communicator. He acted surprised himself and said, "You are so right! It does look like a picture! And I'll bet as the light shadows fall and the colors change, one has a different picture every hour of the afternoon."

Our good communicator did not "up stage" his prospect. He did not move in and take over the conversation, but merely agreed and expanded. He was willing to let her win the Oscar — while he won the sale!

Try this method. It is extremely effective in the art of "Silent Command."

Another Key Principle

Throughout this entire book you will see repeated again and again an emphasis on the principle that people *love to buy* but *hate to be sold*.

Many reasons can be given to support this principle. One of the most important is that when a person is permitted to buy, he is not deprived of the joy of discovery. Furthermore, when a person reaches a conclusion voluntarily and through his own investigation, his decision is usually definite and not subject to easy change. Yes, the decision was his; no one influenced him — he made up his own mind.

How to Communicate Objectively — Not Subjectively

I repeat certain important sentences over and over throughout this book until they have the effect of a broken record. Believe me, it is consciously done and only done for emphasis.

Just a very few sentences carefully used can often make the difference between good and bad communication in the art of "Silent Command."

Five Words of Power

> Mr. Jones, if you could convince yourself that this would help your business, you would have no objection to okaying this purchase order so we can get delivery started at once, would you?

Why is this good communication?

It is communication of the very highest level of persuasion because you are permitting your prospect to act upon his own discovery. Note the magic words, which I urge you to eat, digest and make a part of your everyday vocabulary: *"If you could convince yourself."*

Just these few powerful words can often change what might be considered an effort to sell, yes, even pressure sell, into a polite assistance to one in his buying efforts. These words assure the prospect that he is important, that he is not deprived of the pleasure of acting upon his own good judgment. This is what "Silent Command" is all about.

How to Get the Decision You Want

> Mrs. Smith, based on what you have told me, don't we agree that this is the best thing to do?

Here again we are letting our prospect make the decision. She is kept in the picture and made to feel important. While we bring ourselves into the picture a little more strongly, any decision is based on the discovery the prospect made.

"Low-Pressure" Influencing

Many times when I have wanted to be sure that from the very beginning my respondents realized they would not be deprived of the enjoyment of acting upon their own discovery, I have tried to create the proper climate of communication with some such statement as this:

> Mr. and Mrs. Jones, I want to ask a favor of you. If I should inadvertently say anything that would influence you in the slightest, please call my attention to it, because I want any decision which you may make to be made on your own judgment uninfluenced by me. However, I want to be sure that I give you all the facts so that you can make the right decision.

Now let's analyze the above. How could I be clearer in my assurance that no one would try to high pressure them into anything, that no one would try to deprive them of the pleasure of discovery? However, I also try to make it clear that they will be assisted in their efforts to make a correct decision by being given all the facts.

Do yourself the favor of committing to memory the expressions contained in the last three subheadings of this chapter.

Mental Television Broadcasting

Whenever I face an audience, I am always conscious of the fact that my audience has a very great advantage over me. Each person has complete control over his or her mental television set. I can be turned out at any time. Any person there can switch to another channel of interest. Maybe it's a consideration of their activities the night before. It might even be plans for the coming night. They can be leaning forward and looking at me as though they were listening. Yet they might be on another channel or even unplugged.

When I first began speaking on the circuit, this fact annoyed me. Finally I arrived at the realization that this is part of the protective armor of every audience. It is their standard equipment, their survival kit against the hazards of boring speakers.

Naturally I was concerned with the best method of being sure that I was not tuned out. All the textbooks on public speaking give many methods of capturing an audience's attention at the very start. They list numerous ways to crash that pre-occupational barrier. They assure us that good communication never leaves the starting gate unless we gain that initial attention.

How to Make People Pay Attention to You

Like all other speakers I have read such books and studied the various suggested techniques.

I know one speaker who always appears in a uniform, maybe an umpire's uniform or that of a prisoner. I am sure this is helpful to him in capturing good initial attention. He has a national reputation as an excellent speaker. Another of my friends does a juggler's act. This too must be effective in gaining that first interest because he is well accepted in all circles. I even once saw a speaker who, without saying a word, blew up a balloon and then burst it before a startled audience.

Research shows that our modern circuit speaker is an outgrowth of the medieval juggler, the king's jester and the traveling fiddler. Just to have a message is never enough. One must entertain and provoke attention in order to gain and sustain attention. However, I have found the only true attention getter for me.

Controlling the Communication Climate

After many years of facing an audience I finally learned that it is of little consequence whether my audience thinks that I am an important or a highly successful individual. The point of major concern is the importance with which I regard my audience.

The fact that I truly regard every person in my audience

as being of major importance seems to establish an initial climate of true communication far more effectively than any masquerade I could assume.

The Message in the Eyes

If a speaker on the platform or a person approaching an individual could only realize a certain important principle in communication, he would be much more effective in getting and holding attention.

Please consider this principle carefully. Written in the eyes of every person in my audience and also in the eyes of every respondent you approach, in large neon letters, is the question, "Are you trying to impress me or do you want to help me?"

The Ego Complex

Without being hypercritical of my fellow speakers, I've seen an excellent chairman of the day sell a speaker completely to the audience, only to see the speaker in the initial few minutes buy himself back through an effort to make his audience feel his importance. How different it is when the speaker spends those few minutes making his audience feel important. The ego complex has caused fractured communication for many of us.

How to Create Confidence in You

This principle of causing effective persuasion by making the other fellow feel important has many applications and many variations. A good leader or good executive today is more interested in getting his followers or employees to have confidence in themselves rather than in him. It takes a great deal of unselfishness and interest in other people, but such a quality is the very essence of greatness.

Ideas, however good they may be, are useless unless they

are put into use. For one week, in all your dealings with people let all you say and do communicate clearly the message *"You are important to me."* Don't be startled at the results. Just realize that miracles still do happen!

THIRTEEN

Unleashing the Ultimate Power of Silent Command

We have reached the ultimate in "Silent Command" when we can get people to do what we want them to do because they want to do it. The individuals who are paid most in our economic system are those who have learned the art of causing people to do things. Many people can educate and entertain others, but the real test of a leader is the ability to cause people to do things.

In this chapter I shall remind you of a few qualities that a leader must have. None of them are new to us, but again I say that we need reminding, even of the simplest and most elementary principles. Repetition, repetition, repetition — that's the greatest way of conditioning ourselves to deal with people problems.

ITA Vs. ICA

Have you ever dealt with a person who was smart, polite, and gifted with many good qualities, but you never could feel at ease around him? He appeared brilliant but lacked warmth. For lack of a better expression you labeled him as having the "ivory tower" attitude (ITA). You seemed locked out of his life. You could not get close to him however hard you tried.

On the other hand, have you known people who carried a self-generated warmth and sunshine around with them? You could see from the very beginning that they were interested in you. They simply radiated the "I care" attitude (ICA).

If we desire to learn the art of causing people to do things, to act, we must sincerely have this second attitude.

How a Doctor Becomes Rich

An associate of mine, who recently spoke at a medical convention, related the following story to me.

It appears that he arrived a little early for his speech. An older doctor was talking to a group of interns. According to my associate the older doctor made one of the most profound statements he had ever heard from the medical profession.

He said, "Young fellers, do you know who is the leading doctor in any city? He is not the doctor who is the best surgeon. He is not the doctor who knows the most about medicine. He is the doctor who carries around with him the best "I care" attitude.

Continuing, the doctor said, "Remember this: in 99 cases out of a hundred, regardless of how sick your patients may get, they are going to get well, provided you don't give them something to kill them. Nature is on your side.

"But if, during their sickness, the "I care" attitude is always showing, when they do get well they will swear on a stack of Bibles that through your genius you brought them back from death's door.

"Don't ever speak of a patient as *gall bladder in room 13.* Form the habit of being genuinely interested in your patients and let them know this."

Look at your own sign that you carry around with you. Do you see ITA or ICA?

The Miracle That Takes Only a Few Seconds

Much is said in this book about the art of "Silent Command" and the methods of causing people to obey our wishes, but I cannot emphasize too strongly the importance of that initial approach.

All sales trainers and consultants in the field of human engineering and all those seeking to improve the conduct of others concentrate on the principle that we have no second chance at a first impression. We can correct many mistakes in our interview, but we just can't soften up the cement once it has set.

Remember this: it is in the first few seconds of our interview with a respondent that we put a label on the purpose of our call. We communicate by our words, our actions, and our expression one of two things. We indicate either that we are only there to sell him our proposal, our product or service, or we are there to share valuable ideas and benefits.

The Remarkable Sign

Years ago when I was going from company to company offering a self-improvement course, I had occasion to call on a personnel director who was also purchasing agent for his company.

On his wall he had a sign that I'll never forget. In big bold letters was written "If you show me how your product or service will help me, I shall be even more eager to buy than you are to sell."

This is not just a little fancy sentence. It carries the very essence of good persuasion. If you can communicate to me from the very beginning that you have come to me with ideas to share, ideas that will help me, not just products to unload — "Shoes to get out of the factory" — I shall not even let you leave my office until I have heard your full story.

This Sign Is Always There

This is just as true in other occupations as it is in selling. Get into the habit of mentally seeing that sign just above the head of everyone you call upon, for whatever purpose. Try as hard as you will, you'll find that it is impossible to overwork the words "I have an idea to share with you," "Others have found a great benefit in this," or "This is how our services can increase your business."

Don't forget that the person you call upon is in business to make money. He is interested in your proposal, or your product or service, only to the extent that it will help him make more money. If it does this for him, he wants it, and if it doesn't, he couldn't care less. So shoot the arrow at the bullseye, not out into space.

If you start from the very beginning to talk about your respondent's company, his needs, his problems — not your proposal, your product or your service — you will find that you are oiling the hinges to the door which will quickly open to you.

Every person's favorite subject of discussion is himself and matters that will help him secure the things in life that he wants. Never fear that an initial approach on this subject will not get a responsive note.

Volcanic Spirits

One of the first jobs I ever had was as receptionist for a large food distributing company. Dozens of salesmen called on the company each day. It was interesting to observe the different approaches used, not only upon me to see the buyers, but also upon the buyers themselves.

I remember the method used by one salesman in particular who called upon the company several times a year. He always approached me in a volcanic spirit of excitement, telling me that he had an idea for my boss which couldn't wait. I recall the very words he used on several occasions. He said, "I don't mind waiting, but this idea *can't* wait."

The Great Idea

So aroused was my curiosity that I would always check with the buyer to find out what was the great idea that couldn't wait.

This salesman had made a habit of periodically picking up a plan or an idea which he felt would help his customers — something that had already proved beneficial to others. He was careful to choose an idea that would not help him or his company directly. His initial approach was always to present this plan or idea enthusiastically at the very beginning. The idea was usually good, but the thing that always impressed the buyer most was the fact that it was an unselfish idea — one that was designed to help the buyer, not himself.

To the best of my recollection this particular salesman, during the entire time I worked at that company, never failed to see the person he wanted to see.

The Magic Key That Opens all Doors

This plan of an altruistic approach is certainly not confined to salesmen. Regardless of what you do, you can adapt it. It's a great habit to form. Doors will open to you which you didn't even know existed.

Friends of mine who know that I speak all over the country often tell me of some great idea that I could use in a speech. I'm always interested — never too busy to listen.

Recently a friend of mine heard that I was to speak in Regina, Canada. He called me to tell me a little anecdote that Canadians might appreciate. I was grateful for the story was good and in perfect taste. I used it and it was highly acceptable.

Please never forget that an idea which will help the other person is the magic key that will open the door to any interview.

A Rare Opportunity

During the years as receptionist for the food company to which I referred, I had occasion to study the methods of countless salesmen. While waiting to see the buyers, many would unload their ambitions, aspirations, and even their problems on me. As a receptionist one must learn to be a good listener, a sincere listener, or resign from the job.

I had the rare opportunity to study the thinking and conduct of many of these salesmen who made numerous repeated calls. It was an education in human engineering in general and an education in sales techniques in particular. I'd like to share with you a few observations I made during these years.

The Masked Men Who Failed

I've known "hit-and-run" salesmen. Each time they called it was as though they were making a first call. They had written all over them: "My job is to get the food *out* of the factory — it's a relay race, brother! You take the ball at this point. My responsibility is over. It's up to you now."

While most people mask their faces, these people did an extreme job of it. They had an impersonal expression and manner about them. Their job was to unload a product and then hit the road to the next stop without ever looking back.

Somehow these people didn't seem to last too long. The mortality rate was high.

The Ultimate Consumer

By contrast, I remember vividly those salesmen who seemed even more interested in knowing how our people sold the last order than in making a new sale. They felt a responsibility for their product up to the time it reached the ultimate consumer.

These salesmen didn't feel that the sale was complete until their product had not only reached the retail market but also was in the shopping basket of the consumer.

My memory is much clearer regarding these people because they seemed to be around for years.

Searching the Soul

In looking back and studying salesmen who called at our plant, I must tax my memory to recall the product that some of them sold. I don't mean to imply that they were not good salesmen or were not loyal to their company. The food industry is so highly competitive that the amateurs are eliminated quickly. Also the "pie-in-the-sky, suede-shoe feller" is finished almost before he starts.

But there are some salesmen whom I can hardly separate in my mind from their product. There is old "Corn Flakes Charlie." I can't even remember his last name. He called at least once a week. Everybody loved him. We enjoyed seeing him make his appearance. If his products were not moving fast he hit the ceiling. He wanted to know *why*. If he couldn't get the answer at our office, he would call at the stores to study the situation.

No one in our company objected to the brusque methods of Corn Flakes Charlie. It is true that at times he upset things around our office with his emotional outbursts, but it was only because he loved his products. He wanted to see them sell, and he would help in any way to see that they did move.

Charlie had an expression that I dearly loved. I heard him say more than once, "There's only one thing bad about buying my product; when you buy it you get me too. Furthermore I insist on traveling with that box of cereal all the way to the consumer's breakfast table."

All of us could learn much from Charlie's attitude. Ask yourself, will you, just how much you are a part of your service or product. Does your interest in your product or service end the minute you are paid or do you feel a continuing responsibility? Are you so completely identified with your product or service that people think of you as one? Do a little soul searching at this point.

The Kinesics of the Reception Room

There are some salesmen who have a burning desire to have their product accepted. It is written all over them. They have controlled excitement gleaming in their eyes. Their depth of conviction and urgency of cause is communicated in their manner of conduct. Their very presence generates interest. Such salesmen are an example, not only to other salesmen, but also to those in non-selling occupations.

It was always easy for me to spot such a salesman when he walked up to the reception desk. Furthermore, I was confident that if I tried to slip him into a buyer's office between appointments, he was not going to abuse the privilege.

On the other hand we had our "commercial visitors," too. These people are also an example — an example to avoid.

"I just happened to be in the area and thought I'd drop around and chew the fat with Bill Jones. Is he in?"

Sometimes even when a salesman had an appointment, his entire conduct and demeanor communicated the idea, "I am here just to kill a little time with a buyer so that I can report to my company that I made a call."

It was my job to protect the buyers as best I could against these commercial visitors. Often I would amuse myself by trying to predict in advance whether a salesman was going to get an order or not. I became pretty good at it. Finally it wasn't necessary for me to check with the buyer. The expression on the salesman's face and his general conduct as he left usually communicated to me the information I wanted to know.

Before we go to another point give yourself a little examination. To what extent, whether you sell for a living or not, is your self-image that of a "productive salesman" and to what degree are you just a "commercial visitor"? When you approach a respondent, is it with an appearance of controlled excitement?

Does your manner say, "I can bring a profit to your company with my product. It's a great product. You cannot afford to lose this opportunity"?

Or is your role one of a commercial visitor who, by his complacent attitude, seems to say, "Well, I know I can't win 'em all. Maybe you have an order for me and maybe you don't. But anyway let's see what you might need today."

If you think this is exaggerating, please sit in a reception room where salesmen call on buyers. You will receive a liberal education.

What Does Your Appearance Communicate?

While I am not fastidious about a person's manner of dressing and while I realize that a salesman getting in and out of a car all day cannot forever appear as though he were modeling clothes, his appearance still communicates much about him. This is equally true in other occupations.

If a salesman is carefully groomed, shoes shined, suit pressed, clean shaven, he is in effect saying, "In all I do I am organized and careful over details. If you give me an opportunity to help you, I shall be just as careful and meticulous in handling your affairs."

On the other hand, if the salesman needs a shave and is wearing an unpressed suit, if his collar is frayed and his heels run down, he is communicating just as strongly that he will handle your affairs just as he handles himself. Please, never be licked before you start. At least give yourself a break and not let the interview be born dead because of your appearance.

At times I was horror stricken at the appearance of some salesmen. Their shabby appearance communicated to me that either their product was no good or that they were not good salesmen. In either event I had to protect the buyer from wasting his time with this "joker." If the fellow was worth talking to, he would at least be successful enough to buy a decent suit of clothes and keep himself properly groomed.

How to Please a Woman

Only a few salesmen fully realize how much a receptionist or secretary can help in arranging appointments, even at the last moment, if she really wants to do it.

It's impossible to deal with salesmen month after month and not have your favorites. Furthermore, I must confess that the big sign I mentally wore — *Make me feel important* — never shrank in size during my years as a receptionist.

Somehow I found that I could always be a little more successful in doing favors such as changing appointments and getting interviews for those salesmen who made me feel they considered my position as being important. This, of course, is equally true for persons within a company who wish to see their bosses.

Ready and Willing

No one is exempt from the desire to feel needed. If one feels that another person sincerely needs him and wants help, it is amazing what one is willing to do for that person.

On occasions I have been directly approached in somewhat this manner: "I am in trouble. I perhaps don't deserve your help. However, you are the only one who can help me. Carelessly I didn't make the appointment for this afternoon, but now I find I must fly out tonight. Do you suppose somehow you could help me see Mr. Smith?"

How would you feel if you had an honest approach in this manner? I'm sure you would be moved to help more than if a salesman tried some gimmick or started throwing his weight around.

The Exalted Look

No communication is as persuasive as the exalted look of a believer. It's strange how a person through his manner and expression can cause you to want to open doors for him. A person with a smile and with an attitude of belief in what he is offering radiates an atmosphere of acceptance.

As I say repeatedly throughout this book, "Enthusiasm is more persuasive than logic — excited dedication more moving than all the fancy language that can be concocted."

No statement was ever more true than that which claims that a man dies while he lives if he loses his enthusiasm. I suggest that we all include in our prayers each day, "Dear Lord, please don't let me ever die while I still live — let me die only when I'm dead."

FOURTEEN

Getting Cooperation in Business Through Silent Command

Charles Schwab, the great steel tycoon, once said, "The greatest single quality which contributes to success is the faculty of being able to cause people to cooperate." Many times, however, injustice is done to people. We accuse them of failure to cooperate, when in fact they are more than willing. The truth is that we have not properly communicated to them so that they can cooperate.

Let's examine a few situations where communication is important if we are to get the cooperation we desire.

Secrets of Effective Company Meetings

When people ask the question, "What do you think of company meetings?" it is similar to asking, "How high is up?" or "How deep is down?" It all depends upon the necessity of the meeting, how well we plan it, and the leadership in conducting it and the follow-up.

A meeting can be a costly way of conducting nothing or it can be a very inexpensive way of reaching an objective or solving a problem.

When to Hold the Meeting

Many times a problem concerns only two or three people, not even a whole department. To call a meeting of many employees in such a case as this is clearly as much a waste of time as burning down a house to roast a pig!

Committees which include too many people get less accomplished than single individuals. When the great engineer and executive Charles Kettering was told that Lindbergh had flown the Atlantic, he remarked, "I was always sure that it would never be done by a committee."

I know a certain department head who feels that it gives the employees a sense of importance to be involved in a department meeting. I've discussed these meetings with several of his employees. In many cases those who attend are not involved in the problem nor are they qualified to offer suggestions.

Actually these meetings produce just the opposite of the desired results. Many attending feel left out of the discussion. They feel their time is being wasted. I am sure much more would be accomplished both in problem solving and employee morale if the department head called together only the people involved in each individual problem.

Of course, if a policy matter is to be discussed which involves everyone, this is entirely different. People are more congenial in co-operating and adhering to a policy if they feel that they were taken into confidence and even given a hand in formulating the policy.

How to Plan the Meeting Strategy

If meetings are held too often and are permitted to get out of control "time-wise," they become boring and fail to get the enthusiastic participation which is necessary if they are to justify the time expended. This can be avoided if meetings are called only when necessary and if they are carefully planned in advance.

How to Cover the Vital Points

The effectiveness of many meetings is lost in the maze of incidental points. Meetings which take up the time of a number of people, I again remind you, are costly. Only important matters justify this cost.

If the meeting is scheduled to cover only one or two problems, those attending the meeting should be notified of the agenda in advance. They should be encouraged to give prior thought to the matters which are to come under discussion.

If one person is more involved than others in the matter to be discussed, he in particular should be alerted in time to make special preparation.

If any props are to be used such as slides, charts or flip charts, these should be carefully prepared in advance. They are a most important aid for projecting "Silent Commands."

Proper Direction of the Meeting

The one factor which determines the success of the meeting more than any other is the manner in which the chairman conducts the meeting. Above all else, unless the meeting was called simply to make an announcement — and this is a very expensive way to make an announcement — the chairman should encourage all attending to cooperate and express themselves fully. If one or two people are permitted to monopolize the time, the effectiveness of the meeting suffers.

How to Open the Meeting

A good chairman, regardless of whether those attending have been notified in advance of the objectives of the meeting, will open the meeting with a clear explanation of the purpose for which the members are there.

If certain problems of the company or a department are to be discussed, these should be explained simply. All present should be encouraged to give their ideas as to the best solution. In any group we have people who are reticent about volunteering their ideas. These should be asked to give their ideas, and, if necessary, asked specific questions to help them overcome their hesitancy.

How to Maintain Control of the Meeting

While a good chairman gets as much participation and involvement as seems necessary under the circumstances, he never loses control over the meeting. If a person takes up more time than is advisable, the effective chairman tactfully says something like, "Bill, you have contributed ideas generously. Now I'd like to get the ideas of others. John, how do you feel about the change in our schedule?"

Many people have great difficulty in expressing themselves clearly at a meeting. A good chairman will compliment the person and repeat the point in a more understandable way, saying, "John, I like your idea," and then rephrase the point in clearer terms, giving John the credit for the rephrased idea.

Never should a chairman use such wording as, "What John means is . . .," or "I am sure John is trying to say . . . ." Such an approach is certain to discourage further participation by John.

One of the calculated risks of any meeting is the fact that after a period of time there is a tendency for those present to wander from the objectives of the meeting. It may be that much can be gained from a brief discussion of a few side issues. However, the chairman should always restate the objectives of the meeting after any such side excursion and bring the discussion back to the main points.

Duty of the Chairman

After there has been a full discussion and after decisions have been made, then steps must be taken to act on the decisions. It is the duty of the chairman to summarize the proceedings of the meeting and, where he has authority, delegate certain duties. Otherwise the whole meeting would be futile and a waste of time.

Follow-Up

Just as follow-up and report-back are necessary in any delegation of duties, they are also necessary after such a meeting. Any problem that is important enough to justify a meeting for its discussion is certainly important enough to require a follow-up to make sure that the decisions are carried out.

The next time you have a meeting in your company or department, try following the ideas expressed here. You will find that not only can much time be saved but also better results attained.

Incentive Policies

If a company is to follow the incentive policy in dealing with its employees, it must base both pay and promotion on performance rather than on the number of years worked. A company will have little trouble under such a policy *provided* it has good communication with its employees regarding the manner with which the policy is handled.

Training New People

Many times a supervisor fails to clarify with an employee just what is expected of him. Poor communication regarding job objectives causes breakdown in employee morale from the very beginning.

The most important single step with a new employee is to be sure that he understands completely what is expected of him. A conference should be arranged immediately upon his employment for the specific purpose of discussing his objectives. This should not be a casual conference and the employee should realize the specific purpose of the conference. In this way the employee will remember that his job objectives were clearly defined to him and he will also realize that his supervisor considers them to be important.

Just an explanation by the supervisor is not enough. There should be a thorough discussion with both employer and employee participating. The new employee should be urged to ask questions regarding anything he does not fully understand. He should be told that unless he is fully informed of what is expected of him he can not meet the requirements.

Many good supervisors, in order to take no chances with misunderstanding, will even say something like this: "Mr. Smith, just in order to help you be sure you understand your work objectives I'd like for you to relate to me what your understanding is of your duties."

How to Get Maximum Performance

In order to get the maximum performance from an employee, this employee must feel that his work is periodically analyzed. It is very difficult for an employee to take pride in the quality of his work over any prolonged period of time if he feels that shoddy work is overlooked and good performance is not recognized.

Reviewing and Evaluating Work

Any worthwhile employee not only wants his work evaluated but he also wants the supervisor to discuss his work with him. Every employee has a right to know where he stands with his company. If his work is satisfactory, he feels he should be told that it is. He feels entitled to a pat on the back. If his work is unsatisfactory, he also feels that he has a right to this report. He even feels that he should be told exactly in what way he did not measure up and coached on the manner in which he can improve his performance.

A good supervisor will keep a written report on each man for whom he is responsible. When evaluating an employee's work with him he should have this report in front of him. Not only is this the fair and accurate way of employee appraisals, but it also impresses the employee. He knows that any evaluation prepared over a period of time is more accurate than a mere discussion off the top of one's head

What Is the Yardstick in Judging Me?

Just to be absolutely certain that there is full communication with the employee regarding his job analysis, it is well to discuss with him the yardstick with which he is to be judged.

Many companies use different factors in judging their employees and some put greater stress upon certain qualities than others. However, the following or some variation of these are found in most job analysis programs:

How devoted is the employee in seeing that the general purposes of his company are carried out?

What is the volume and quality of the work produced?

How accurate is the employee in following company policies as well as specific instructions?

Can this employee be depended upon to complete the job assigned on the schedule given?

Is this employee a self-starter and always prompt or does he require constant supervision after the assignment has been made?

Within the scope of his particular job is his thinking clear and his judgment sound?

Are his relations with his fellow employees harmonious? In other words, is he a team worker or an individualist?

If he deals with the public, what impression does he make? Does he communicate a good company image?

Making People Feel Involved

If my duties are accurately defined to me and if you periodically sit down with me and discuss my progress with the company, not only do I feel that my work is not being ignored but I feel involved in the company.

Please don't fail to criticize me constructively where criticism is due. If the only appraisal of my work is complimentary, I have no opportunity to improve myself. Furthermore, when you include both praise *and* criticism I feel that you are truly interested in seeing that I progress.

How to Fire People Without Bitterness

If I am called in suddenly and told that my work is unsatisfactory and that I am no longer with the company, I would resent such treatment.

However, if over a period of time I have been first reminded of shortcomings, then urged and finally warned about these faults, and furthermore if I had not corrected them, then my termination would certainly come as no surprise. I could not be bitter or feel that I had not been given ample opportunity to improve the quality of my work.

Giving Instruction Attractively

We have heard the old cliché, "It's not what you say but how you say it," so long that many of us consider it too "corny" to repeat. However, this is very true in the field of giving instructions. A supervisor who has the gift of having people do things because they want to do them is truly a magician; this power is magic.

I remember an instance which occurred when I was receptionist. It was Friday afternoon about closing time. I had experienced a strenuous week and I was eager to get home.

The president of our company rushed by my desk, dropped a file on it, and said, "I'm trying to catch a plane. This must be in the mail by midnight. I haven't time to explain. A letter of explanation is attached."

It is mild to say that I hit the ceiling. The week was up. I had worked hard. My plans for the evening had already been set. Why was it up to me to concern myself over this matter? Just how thoughtless could anyone be!

I started cleaning up my desk to leave for the weekend. I promised myself I was not going to touch the file even if it meant losing my job. Finally, as I was ready to go, I opened the file. I assure you it was out of curiosity and not with the slightest idea of doing anything about it.

There on top was a hurriedly scribbled note: "Merlyn, I am in real trouble. There is no excuse for what I did. How

I forgot this I'll never know. As you realize, this is our biggest account. It's a great imposition on you. Not only are you the only one I'd trust with this but you are the only one sweet and unselfish enough to help me out of this predicament. Please forgive me — I'll make it up to you in some way."

What would you have done? I'm sure — the same as I.

Yes, in the pleasure of feeling important and needed I lost any resentment. The important letter was in the mail by six-thirty and I kept my engagement. If necessary I would have worked all night, however.

Can you make your employees feel needed and important? It's unbelievable what a supervisor can get his employees to do and even do cheerfully, if only he uses the right approach.

Examples of Good and Bad Communication

Let's just look at a few examples of good and bad communication on the part of supervisors. When conducting clinics in the field of communication, I usually ask one lady to help in a little role playing. We name her Negative Nell. I then ask two men to volunteer. We call them the Positive Supervisor and the Negative Supervisor.

The three come to the platform. I hand each some material to read and ask them to "ham it up" and put real showmanship in their parts. Not only do these people usually turn out to be entertaining but they put over the message in a way that it's not forgotten.

Now let's review a few of these skits.

Overworked

Negative Nell: I can't get all this work done in just eight hours.

Negative Supervisor: The other girl did.

You can imagine what Nell's reaction would be to this statement by her supervisor. Now consider what a people-oriented supervisor would have said:

Positive Supervisor: Which part of your work do you
feel is the most urgent?

Now Nell begins to talk about the work. The Long Acre account can't be neglected. The Ford job is urgent. Maybe Nell will arrive, through her own reasoning, at the conclusion that nothing can be neglected. At least her judgment has been considered.

Where to Put the Files

Negative Nell: Let's get rid of some of these files.
Negative Supervisor: We can't. We use them daily.

What do you suppose a supervisor who is a human engineer would have said?

Positive Supervisor: Where do you think would be a
better location for them?

Now Nell begins to consider alternatives. They can't be put in the stock room; that's overcrowded. Certainly they can't be hauled to the basement. That's been flooded twice. Nell finally, upon her own volition, decides that perhaps there is no better place for them than where they are.

Old-Fashioned Method

Negative Nell: This method is old-fashioned and out of
date.
Negative Supervisor: That's the way we have always
done it.

How much better it would have been if the following answer had been given:

Positive Supervisor: What method would you suggest?

Maybe Nell can suggest a better method. If so she will be helpful and happy as well. If not, it will finally occur to her that it's not a good policy to criticize unless you have first arrived at a better way of doing something.

Not My Responsibility

Negative Nell: It's not *my* responsibility.
Negative Supervisor: Well, somebody's got to do it.
Positive Supervisor: Who do you think should be responsible?

Now Nell brings her own reasoning into the picture. Mary can't do it; she's snowed under. Ethel is too new and inexperienced. Nell finally decides that perhaps, after all, she's the one to do it.

How Urgent?

Negative Nell: How soon do I have to have this done?
Negative Supervisor: It should have been done two hours ago.

How much cooperation do you think that answer is going to get from Nell?

Positive Supervisor: When would it be possible to have it completed?

Here the supervisor has given Nell an opportunity to take pride in her own performance. Nell can declare herself a fast worker or a slow worker. At least Nell feels that she has been given consideration.

I Don't Like the Program

Negative Nell: I don't think it's a good program and I don't have the time to get involved.
Negative Supervisor: I guess you'll just have to *take* the time.

What does our people-oriented supervisor say?

Positive Supervisor: Why do you think this would not be
a good program?

The Six Most Useful Words for Supervisors

Did you notice the common denominator of every answer by the Positive Supervisor? He answered every time with a question, the most powerful way to communicate if we want to get cooperation.

Six of the most useful words for any supervisor to remember are *who, what, when, which, where* and *why*. These are six honest working words that will help him tremendously in his communication with employees if he will only remember to use them. The Positive Supervisor started every question with one of these words. I am sure you noticed this.

I hope this chapter will convince you that good communication is the essence and nucleus of good cooperation. It is almost unbelievable, unless you have researched the matter, to find how many people fail to cooperate, not because they lack loyalty but because they lack understanding. Also we find that many supervisors invite lack of cooperation because they are not people-oriented in their communication. Please be careful in all your people transactions to communicate clearly. Good communication breeds good cooperation; faulty communication generates lack of cooperation.

FIFTEEN

How to Handle
Specific Situations
with Silent Command

There are many transactions, performances and events in which we are involved that depend for their success upon good communication. To say that persuasive communication is simple but not easy appears to be a contradiction within itself. But actually this statement is very true. If a few basic principles of communication are thoroughly understood and followed meticulously, what might appear to be a difficult task often becomes the essence of simplicity.

This chapter might be considered a reference chapter. If you are called upon to do any of the things illustrated in this chapter and if you study the contents and follow the suggestions, you will find little difficulty in your task. In fact, you will take joy in the participation.

How to Introduce a Speaker

Please do not be concerned with the long lists given in many textbooks on the subject, of things to do and to remember when you introduce a speaker. Just the volume of information is enough to frighten many people from the task.

Actually there are only three important steps. If you forget all else and stick to these three, you will perform your

169

task well and have the gratitude of your audience and *especially* of your speaker.

Importance of the Subject

Everyone enjoys taking part in an important event. It helps our ego and we attack the task with enthusiasm.

Especially is this true in the field of speech-making. If I am the speaker and I hear my chairman tell of the importance of my subject, I feel inspired to treat the important subject with care and excellence of performance. Also, such an approach sharpens the interest of the audience.

Yes, the first step in a good introduction is for the chairman to sell the audience initially on the fact that the subject is of utmost importance.

Particularly Important to This Audience

The next step brightens the opportunity of the speaker and lifts the event to an even greater level by telling why the subject is of great importance to this particular audience.

If the subject is sales and the audience consists of salesmen, this is very easy. If the audience is comprised of industrial workers and the subject is safety, again it is a simple matter. However, sometimes we must use our imagination and creative ability to take this second step.

Especially Qualified Speaker

The first two steps are, in reality, only preparation for the third step. In this third step we qualify the speaker for the task he is about to perform. We iterate his qualifications, experience, and training which make him an expert on his subject.

The method of presenting a speaker is elementary. Don't burden yourself with anything other than these three steps. They must follow in logical sequence, as listed. Each is related to the other and each has a particular task to be performed.If you follow this pattern, you cannot fail to be impressive in your introductions.

Now let's examine an example of the proper method of presenting a speaker.

A Model Introduction

Let's imagine that I am asked to introduce a speaker. The occasion is a banquet of safety engineers. The speaker is a specialist in the field of accident prevention.

> Members of our Safety Engineering Society and honored guests. The subject of safety is of great importance throughout the entire world.
>
> The fact is that the dignity of man, the freedom of life and the worship of God in all lands and in all times have never been any greater than the importance which the people of that particular nation put upon the safety and sanctity of life of the individual.
>
> This subject of safety is of particular interest to us here tonight, because in our profession we have dedicated our lives to accident prevention and to promoting standards of safety.
>
> There is no man in America today who is better qualified to bring us a message on safety than our guest speaker tonight.
>
> Jim Riley has been a professor of instruction and research on safety at M.I.T. for over 15 years. He has set up the safety program in many of our nation's largest industries. His great book *Life, Liberty and the Pursuit of Safety* is the bible in the safety department of practically every large company today.
>
> Those of you who have had the privilege of hearing Dr. Riley realize what a treat you have in store. To those of you who have not heard him I congratulate you on your good fortune here this evening.
>
> I now introduce Dr. Jim Riley, who will address you on the subject "Are Accidents Really Necessary?"

I cannot conceive of any circumstance which should call

for an introduction any longer than this one. All three bases were touched — the importance of the subject, the special importance to that particular audience, and finally the qualifications of the speaker.

Prostituting an Introduction

I've never heard a speaker complain about an introduction being too brief. However, nothing is more discouraging to a speaker than to be so unfortunate as to be inflicted with a chairman who prostitutes an introduction into an opportunity to render an oration.

Every speaker has had this unfortunate experience on at least one occasion. Mine came early in my speaking career. I was to address a convention banquet. The hour was late. The "Happy Hour" which preceded the banquet went about an hour overtime. Business and election of officers ran far over the time anticipated, and it was after ten o'clock when the program began.

The president apologized for the lateness of the hour and politely suggested that perhaps we should cut the program down in time. This suited me as I observed that the audience was almost in a coma.

Finally the chairman arose to introduce me. For exactly 23 minutes by my watch he told jokes, referred to remarks of other speakers over the years, and related the efforts that he and two pals of his had exerted eight years earlier in organizing the association. Eventually, when he was exhausted, he simply said, "And now it is my duty to introduce the speaker. Her qualifications and subject were contained in a bulletin sent you last week, and now here she is — let's bring her on with applause."

I carefully gave my name, spelled it, and then gave my subject and spoke for 18 minutes and sat down.

The wonderful audience gave me one of the most spontaneous standing ovations I have ever received. I am confident it was provoked through sympathy over my introduction and appreciation of my brevity.

The Rule of Brevity

Please don't think that I meant to imply that all or even most of the chairmen violate the rule of brevity in making introductions. However, we do have a few frustrated people who grasp the opportunity of chairmanship just to get before the public and expound their views.

Actually, if a person is a compulsive speaker, he should never accept the job of making an introduction. Some people simply can't restrain themselves while on the platform. Just as we have drug addicts and alcohol addicts, we have speaking addicts. If you are one, don't accept the job of introducing a speaker. One must be very unselfish to do the job well. The person introducing is merely the frame around the picture. He is there to make the speaker look good, not to up-stage him.

If he tells a joke or gives any matter of substance, he is taking away from the speaker. Of course, if the job is that of master of ceremonies, that is a different matter. I am referring here to the person whose sole job is to introduce the speaker. He should follow the three steps as outlined and restrict himself to just that role. Even if the master of ceremonies introduces the speaker, when he reaches that point, he, too, should reduce his activities to the pattern of the three steps.

In contrast to the 23-minute oration by the person who was to introduce me, I remember vividly an experience I had recently before the Greater Vancouver Real Estate Board in Canada. I was to give a two-hour seminar on communication as applied to real estate selling. I am sure I never had a nicer introduction and I say confidently it was the shortest.

In a crisp English accent, the chairman, to the best of my recollection, merely said,

> Lack of understanding and faulty communication is responsible for most of the world's troubles today. To those of us in real estate selling the subject of good communications is doubly important because without it we cannot survive. We have with us today America's

leading speaker on this subject. Mrs. Merlyn Cundiff has spoken in six foreign countries, written a book and made numerous records all in the field of communications. I now introduce Mrs. Merlyn Cundiff who will speak on the A.B.C. of selling — Always Be Communicating."

The Element of Surprise

Elsewhere in this book we elaborated on the destructive aspect of removing the element of surprise.

This principle applies in introduction of a speaker also. While we want to qualify a speaker in the third step of our introduction, we can often handicap his chances if we are too complimentary.

Give his qualifications but let him prove his own case. If the speaker is good, his audience is sure to find it out. If he is not, all the flamboyant compliments are not going to help his case.

Relationship Between Chairman and Speaker

I spoke to an organization on "Bosses' Night." At the time I was asked to speak I was told that the whole climate of the meeting should be one of levity and consequently I should not present any serious ideas but treat the occasion lightly. Though I do not consider myself a joke teller I agreed to speak with tongue in cheek and refrain from any heavy material.

Imagine my chagrin when a person I had never seen before, but who must have received his instructions somewhere, started introducing me in this vein: "This is a night for fun — not anything serious. Consequently we have invited a person to come here tonight and tell us a lot of jokes. If she is as funny as I hear she is she will have you rolling in the aisles. I now present your entertainer, Mrs. Cundiff."

Such a breakdown in communication as this can be disastrous to a speaker. If you are the chairman, take nothing for granted. Check your introduction with the speaker. It is a *must* if you want to avoid such experiences as the one stated above.

I am sure you are wondering if I escaped the ordeal mentioned above without battle scars. Though horrified at first over my predicament, I changed my subject to "Humorous Breakdowns in Communication." After 20 minutes of reciting impossible incidents of embarrassment arising out of fractured communication, I analyzed my own introduction as the breakdown of communication to end all breakdowns!

My audience was with me that night. I was thankful for my escape. However, I made a resolution which I have kept since that incident. If the chairman does not check with me regarding my introduction I always check with him, however clumsy may be the situation.

Platform Kinesics

When you introduce a speaker, never leave the podium until the speaker arrives at it. Then when he is only a few feet away, step back graciously and give the speaker your position. Never leave a podium unattended even for two seconds.

An unattended podium not only creates a bad impression with the audience but also puts the speaker at a disadvantage. The warmth of an introduction, however good, is lost and the spell broken when the podium is left unattended even momentarily.

If your speaker must walk up from the audience, stand by your guns and don't leave your post until he arrives. It is a courteous thing to do; your audience will like it and your speaker will be grateful.

Recently I had to walk up from the audience and the chairman and I had a two-person traffic jam on the steps to the stage. It was a clumsy situation and everyone was embarrassed unnecessarily.

You may never have occasion to introduce a speaker, but if the opportunity ever arises don't be afraid to accept it. You now know the fundamentals. You can't go wrong. Just as a matter of interest the next time you witness an introduction, note whether the chairman touches the three bases or whether he appropriates the occasion for the purpose of making a speech himself.

How to Present a Trophy or Plaque

If you are a member of any club, organization or association, chances are that you have many occasions to witness the presentation of a certificate, cup or trophy. You may even be called upon to make the presentation yourself. Good communication requires that this be done according to a simple and definite pattern. A straight line is the shortest distance between two points. So why race all around the world to arrive at the house next door?

As guest speaker at a sportsman's banquet I once heard a very interesting story concerning this question asked of Howard Hill, the great bow-and-arrow expert: "Mr. Hill, other people go hunting with high-powered rifles and the best equipment money can buy. Their percentage of success is very small. You, however, use only a bow and arrow, and yet, I understand, it is very rare that you return without your game. How is this possible?"

His answer was this: "I study my game's eating, sleeping and feeding habits. Then I plan my hunt with infinite care and follow these plans with utmost precision. If I did otherwise, I would not be hunting at all. I would only be walking in the woods."

Unfortunately too many people, in presenting a trophy, do not plan this important undertaking — they are merely "walking in the woods."

Now let's learn a little simple formula which will insure our being a master communicator in making such a presentation.

Four Points of the Presentation

Remember these four simple points that must be made clear if the presentation is to be professional in its nature. They should not be out of order:

1. The person responsible for the presentation.
2. The reason it is being given.
3. What the recipient did to earn it.
4. The actual presentation.

The actual presentation, which should occur only *after* the first three points are covered, should be made gracefully and as a concluding gesture. I'm sure all of us have seen the actual handing over of the trophy or cup before or during the speech of presentation. This destroys the dramatic effect.

If I drank a toast to an individual or to an occasion with a few well-chosen words, the incident would be clumsy and futile if I drank the toast before or during my words. No, I conclude my remarks and *then* drink the toast. Maybe you feel that this admonition is unnecessary. If you think so, just watch carefully the next few such presentations. I regret to predict that you will probably see many violations of this principle. A good presentation is thus spoiled unnecessarily.

Example of Presentation

Note the four points in the following presentation:

> Each year your Chamber of Commerce gives a plaque of honor to one of its members. *(Point #1.)*
>
> This plaque is given to the member who has, during the previous 12 months, been most active in chamber affairs. *(Point #2.)*
>
> Harry Smith, because of the many hours spent in chamber work and because of his outstanding work as head of the membership committee, has been selected by the awards committee to be the recipient of this plaque. *(Point #3.)*

It gives me pleasure to present this plaque to you, Mr. Smith, in behalf of your chamber, because of your outstanding work. *(Point #4.)*

The above is not complicated, is it? Please refer to it in the event you are to make a presentation some day. You can relate it to any occasion. It is simple and straight to the point.

How to Accept a Trophy or Plaque

If we picked the one platform occasion where more violations of good communication are made than any other, it would be the occasion of a trophy acceptance. We should not be critical but should be very forgiving in this instance.

In the first place in many cases the recipient is caught by surprise, and does not have time to ponder over the occasion or to arrange his thoughts or words. Very few people are at ease in delivering an impromptu speech.

Even if the recipient suspected that he would receive the award, in many cases he is so overcome by emotion that he cannot speak. This is not detrimental to him. A sincere display of unavoidable emotions is often far more impressive and communicates appreciation more articulately than anything that can be said.

But if you want to be able to say the proper thing in your acceptance of a trophy or certificate just analyze these three little points. It will insure a brilliant speech of acceptance every time.

1. Thank the person presenting the trophy.
2. Then thank the club, association or company responsible for the trophy.
3. Finally, as you fondle the trophy or cup affectionately, tell the group what you plan to do with it.

Now let's see how Harry Smith would accept the plaque presented to him at the Chamber of Commerce Banquet.

> Thank you, Ray Thomas. *(Point #1.)* My deepest ap-
> preciation to my chamber for this honor. *(Point #2.)*
> I shall hang this plaque on the wall of my office where
> I can see it every day and each time I look at it I shall
> remember my many friends who made this presentation
> possible. *(Point #3.)*

There is nothing complicated about the above. If you
understand these three little points you can give an impromptu speech of acceptance any time. The fact is that it
is bad taste to make such an acceptance speech too long.

Now that you understand this method of acceptance, I am
sure that I could wake you up at three in the morning, make
a presentation to you, and you could give a brilliant acceptance speech with only ten seconds of preparation.

It is good taste on the part of a recipient of an award to
share the honors with any one or more people who may have
assisted him. For instance, Harry Smith could have said, just
after thanking Ray Thomas, who made the presentation:

> I accept this plaque in behalf of myself and the
> devoted members of the membership committee who are
> responsible for the membership increase of our chamber.
> *(Point #1.)*
> We all thank the chamber for this presentation.
> *(Point #2.)* I shall hang the plaque on the wall of my
> office where I can see it every day and each time I
> look at it, I shall remember the great cooperation on
> the part of the members of my committee and my many
> friends in the chamber who made this presentation
> possible. *(Point #3.)*

One of the unpardonable sins of trophy acceptance is to
begin an acceptance speech by saying that you don't deserve
the honor. You may have the best of intentions in such a
remark, but it is "speech suicide," the oratorical equivalent
to a blocked punt. It is almost as bad as starting a regular
speech with an apology. The numerous reasons are too
obvious to need explanation.

The Use of Exhibits

The proper use of an exhibit can add to practically every speech. Exhibits are dangerous, however, to an inexperienced speaker because exhibits if used improperly detract from a speech and in some cases can prove fatal.

Before demonstrating the proper use of an exhibit, let's analyze the reason an exhibit can be effective.

In the field of communication we are concerned with many factors which are involved in stimulus and response. No single one is more effective than sight. Consequently when we can add this factor to our oral presentation, we are increasing our communication considerably, using one of the most effective "Silent Command" techniques.

There is also a benefit to the speaker. When we can hold up an exhibit or present a picture on the screen; we are often more natural and more effective. We are never bothered with the handicap of self-consciousness. Consequently a person who is bothered by this self-consciousness will find great comfort in exhibits. Even his own attention is diverted from himself and directed toward the exhibit.

In the proper use of an exhibit there are a few principles which must be followed. If you don't use these principles, not only will you fail to get any benefit from the exhibits but also they will detract from any good communication you might have had without them.

Let's start with the major premise that exhibits are not very forgiving of improper use. You can't afford even to consider them unless you adhere to the principles communicated herein.

How to Reveal an Exhibit

Nothing is more distracting to an audience than to observe an exhibit which the speaker has half-hidden and half-revealed. Their curiosity is excited but not satisfied. We can be sure of only one thing. The audience is too interested in mystery to concentrate on anything the speaker might be saying.

The exhibit should be brought to the podium and put out of sight either before the speaking starts or during a coffee break or recess. Any elaborate exhibit brought to the podium while an audience is present, even if put out of sight after arriving, has done its destructive work. The audience will be on pins and needles wondering when it will be revealed.

An exhibit must be handled with the skill of a magician. At the time of its use, quickly and gracefully see that it makes its appearance.

Appearance and Disappearance

Unless you can see that the exhibit is capable of a disappearing act after its use, don't use it in the first place. If the exhibit lingers after it has served its purpose, it will only be a distracting factor to the audience. Don't compete with your exhibit for attention. It will be your friend and help you if you will let it, but it also can work to your detriment.

How to Build Up the Exhibit's Importance

In the event that the exhibit is one you can hold up, be sure to hold it delicately and respectfully out from you and only glance at it when you are calling attention to some feature of it. The proper use of an exhibit is not hard to perfect if you follow instructions and practice proper performance.

If you haven't noticed before, please observe carefully the next time you see a speaker use an exhibit. Unfortunately, in the majority of cases the speaker will direct his entire attention to the exhibit and ignore his audience. One would think he was making a speech to the exhibit.

Only one thing is worse than speaking to the exhibit and that is holding it in front of you and not out to the side. I've seen speakers hold a large card up in front of them so that they appeared to be "sandwich men." I've even seen them hold cards in front of their faces, thereby hiding themselves.

Regardless of what the exhibit is, treat it as though it were invaluable. Almost caress it — move it gently about. Your audience will not consider it of any greater importance than that which you give to it.

How to Use Notes

People are forever asking me at clinics and seminars on effective speaking whether or not the use of notes detracts from a speech.

The answer is the same as with so many things. It all depends on the manner in which you handle the situation. If you feel more comfortable with notes, I would urge you by all means to use them but to take the time to learn how to use them properly.

Have notes readily available. They should be kept on the podium in front of you where they can be seen at all times. If there is no podium, then have them in your hand.

When you refer to them, if they are on the podium just glance down; never bend over or duck your head to see them. If they are too far away, then pick them up and hold them out proudly with your head high as you refresh your memory or get your next cue.

Never give the impression that you are slyly trying to refresh your memory without letting your audience see you do it. Actually your audience has no objection to notes properly used, but if it feels you are not letting them in on the reference, then it seems "sneaky."

If ever you step away from the podium and then step back for the purpose of referring to your notes, you have made too big of a thing of it. You give the impression that you have forgotten your subject and are desperately trying to refresh your memory so that you can get back on the right track. Guard against this.

By the same token never try to hide your notes as a magician would, or make them disappear. Again, most audiences are fair provided you are fair with them.

Handling Notes on the Platform

When you do refer to notes which you are holding in your hand, bring your hand out and up, so that you can glance at them. Don't bend over or nod your head. Treat your notes respectfully and handle them gently. They are gems of wisdom you are carrying proudly to your audience — not a crutch to assist your memory.

How to Give Prestige to a Speech

I attended a conference which was addressed by a college president. He used notes but did so very skillfully.

On one occasion he said, "My next point I considered to be so important that I wrote it down to be sure I wouldn't overlook it."

He proudly held his notes out in front of him as he looked at them. In my own mind I felt that here was a man who considered his audience so important that he had prepared his subject matter. Furthermore, I could hardly wait to hear what the important point was to which he had referred.

At another point in his speech he quoted a certain person. As he glanced at his notes he said, "I considered this quotation a spark of genius and I wanted to be sure I quoted it exactly. So I wrote it down and I'll now read it to you."

I am sure no one could object to the use of notes in this manner. In fact, it gave authenticity and prestige to the entire speech.

Substitute Mental Notes

I am one of many speakers who, in their mind's eye, place imaginary words or figures on the walls of the auditorium to insure themselves of no breakdown in memory. It is a very easy thing to do. The more ridiculous the figure or little character, the less are your chances of forgetting. I sometimes go to the auditorium or other meeting place early in order that I can have time to fix the little figures indelibly in my memory. It may seem corny and overly simple, but it has the homely virtue of working.

Your ability to introduce a person, to present or accept a trophy, or even to use an exhibit properly will not alter the course of history or materially change your life. These are, however, useful skills to have, and can be easily mastered if you follow the elementary principles given in this chapter. Through continued practice of these principles you will find your ability to communicate is greatly increased.

SIXTEEN

The Lifetime Plan for Silent Command Power Development

Since we all agree that we are communicating all of our waking hours and since some of us even feel that by our body positions and movements we are communicating while asleep, doesn't it seem well to consider just how effectively we communicate during our 24 hours?

By relating yourself to a day's communication you can guard against the purely academic approach. Be sure to apply these principles to your everyday experience.

This chapter is going to explain a Lifetime Plan for Silent Command Power development. It will show you how you can start strengthening this power within you from the time you wake up in the morning, throughout your busy day at work, and for week after week, month after month, year after year, reaching and maintaining your powers at their full peak as long as you need them.

On Waking Up

It has been said that every person wakes up each morning to a world of his own making. What do we really mean by the old expression that we "got up on the wrong side of the bed today"?

A person upon awakening can communicate two things. He can get up eager to start the day. By his very manner he can say, "This is a great day — something wonderful is going to happen. In fact, I shall go out and make it happen." On the other hand, by his actions he can communicate, "I hope this day is no worse than yesterday."

I once heard a person relate that as we open our eyes each morning we silently say either "Good morning, God" or "Good God, it's morning."

It is very important to start out each day in a happy mood, figuratively standing tip-toe with expectation. If we feel this way, we communicate this feeling to all those around us. Just as an experiment, take an inventory of yourself tomorrow morning when you wake up. What image do you communicate?

Stoplights and Go-Lights

Are you relaxed as you drive to your work? If not, try relaxing. I promise you that a rigid, nervous person under a strain does not arrive at the office any sooner than one who takes everything in stride and rolls with the punches.

The intersection lights are put there to help speed up the traffic and get you to where you are going faster and with less congestion. In reality, we should speak of the traffic lights not as "stoplights" but as "go-lights."

Recently I stopped at a filling station in a large city and asked for directions to a certain auditorium. The attendant told me to go down to the third red light and turn to the left; two blocks from this red light would be the auditorium.

I was tempted to say, "Do you mean the third red light or the third green light?" But I was sure I would only congeal my own confusion still further.

Starting with the Right Attitude

The next time you observe a car waiting for the traffic light to change, notice how often you will see the driver glance up and down at the red light nervously. What do you think he is communicating? He is perhaps saying, "In this mad, wild, fitful, feverish life I can hardly afford to wait one minute for anything. If I keep looking up and down, maybe the light will change quicker."

Ponder a little on your own actions. Do you communicate to the person driving the car next to you that you have fallen into the "hurry, worry, bury" attitude of life?

Secret of Controlled Excitement

Now you are at your office and ready to face your day of work. What does your approach to your tasks express? Is it one of controlled excitement? Remember, I said that the richest person on this earth is the person who is having a love affair with his job. He is rich because he never drudges another day of his life. His activities constitute pleasure. His job is not just a source of income; it is a source of satisfaction and fulfillment. Lucky indeed is the person who finds excitement in what he is doing.

When is the last time you asked yourself just what it is that motivates you to follow your business, industry, or profession? If it's money alone that we are working for, we are underpaid. To feel chained to a job only for the sake of making a living is indeed a miserable situation. If you cannot find other satisfactions in your work besides just the income, you owe it to yourself to search for something else that *can* offer pleasure, excitement, and a challenge.

Take This Simple Test

Suppose that you are now busy at work with your fellow employees. The very success of your company's production depends on good communication. The art of communication is just as important to you whether you give or receive instructions. Remember, I emphasized from the very beginning that communication is a two-way street. Both the communicator and the respondent must be in complete harmony.

Think back over the last few weeks and try to remember if there has been a breakdown in communication where you were involved. If you can recall such an instance, try to analyze the situation and arrive at the cause of the misunderstanding. If you were part of the error, was the mistake made because of inarticulate speaking or because of careless listening?

An Ancient Doctrine

In law there is a doctrine called *contributory negligence.* One is not permitted to collect damages from a negligent person involved in an accident if the complaining party contributed to the accident by being negligent also. If I see a person driving carelessly toward me, and although I have plenty of time to avoid an accident by taking reasonable precautions I do not take them, then I cannot collect damages because in the sight of the law I contributed to the accident.

I feel that this same doctrine holds true in the field of communication.

The Blind Spots

Imagine that my supervisor calls me into his office and assigns to me a certain task to be performed. My supervisor at this time is under extreme pressure and radiates this nervousness to me. Observing how busy he is, I do not wish to take up any more of his time than necessary. Consequently I do not ask as many questions about the assignment as I would have asked if I had felt my supervisor had more time to spend with me.

When I approach the assigned task I now find many blind spots in my understanding of the job. I am faced with two alternatives. I can either take a chance on doing the job in a manner that may not comply with the way my supervisor wants it done or I can go back and ask for more instructions.

If I adopt the former, I am taking a chance which might turn out to be costly. It's strange that although a person often feels that he doesn't have time to do a job right he always has to find time to do it over if it is not done correctly.

If I proceed along the second course, then I can be sure that the sum total of time of the two meetings with my supervisor is more than would have been expended if I had asked many questions and insisted on clarification of those things I did not understand when first I was given instructions.

Radiation of Emotions

Now let's be honest about the communication by my supervisor and also by me. A person cannot afford to be too busy to give instruction clearly and understandably. If my supervisor was too busy to give instructions clearly, he should not have attempted to give them in the first place. He should have waited until he had more time. Again I say that if a person is under a strain, he radiates that emotion to his listener who also becomes nervous. Instructions, to be given correctly, must be given slowly and in a relaxed manner.

My supervisor should have taken the time to ask me questions to find out if I clearly understood the project. If there were a doubt in his mind, he could have even asked me to repeat to him my understanding of what I was to do.

Yes, my supervisor was clearly in error. He could have taken out insurance against misunderstanding by asking me questions and requesting that I repeat to him my understanding of my job. So I feel that we can safely say that in every case of lack of understanding the supervisor is not without blame.

Understanding Your Duties

The fact that my supervisor failed to make himself clear does not free me from blame. In no instance should I tackle a job assigned to me until I fully understand my duties. It might be embarrassing to me at times. I may not want to appear stupid. But it is not mentally honest for me to proceed until, in my own mind, I have a complete understanding of what I am to do.

From the point of view of what I owe to my company, it is not right for me to fail to stand my ground and insist on complete understanding, and furthermore, it will bring more embarrassment to me. And so I feel that we can safely say that in every case of lack of understanding the person receiving instructions is not without blame.

How to Avoid Being a Victim

On first impression you might feel that in the field of fractured communication it is unfair to indict both parties, but I disagree. I repeat that both parties have a method of taking out insurance against faulty understanding. This insurance lies in the activity of questioning.

All the supervisor in the above instance was required to do, if he wanted to take out insurance against lack of understanding, was to propound a series of questions. This would easily have revealed whether there was proper understanding or not. By the same token, if I do not fully understand instructions, I am only required to ask questions regarding things that are not fully clear to me.

Let's adopt the principle that no one is the innocent victim of errors because of faulty instructions given in the presence of a person who has the opportunity to ask questions. This may be a harsh indictment, but if we are to hold high standards in the field of communication we cannot in complete honesty take any other stand.

The Perfect "Out"

Suppose that my instructions from my supervisor were to call upon a certain person, a prospective client, to offer the services of our company. In this instance his instructions were clear; there was no breakdown in communication.

I call my prospective client for an appointment. Remember that in seeking the physical interview I only want to sell the importance of listening — not my services. This has been emphasized elsewhere in this book. I can't be too emphatic about it.

Again, one of the principal reasons for a person's failure

to give another an appointment is that he feels that in so doing
he is in some small way committing himself to accept the
product or service when offered. To guard against this I am
very careful not even to mention the features or benefits
of anything I have to offer when making the appointment.
If necessary I even go further than this. I give the prospective
client a perfect "out" without any embarrassment if he does
not wish to accept our services.

> Mr. Jones, I have no idea at all whether you are inter-
> ested in our services or not. You can decide very easily
> after hearing me. However, I do have some very valuable
> information about our services which might prove most
> important and beneficial to you. I'd like to know when
> it's most convenient for you to receive this information.
> May I come over at three this afternoon, or would an
> earlier time be more convenient for you?

The Most Effective Tool

Used correctly, the multiple choice of "yes" is one of the
most effective tools in the art of communication and persuasion. However, if we are crude or too obvious about it,
we can cause resentment in the other party. The whole
theory of its effectiveness is based on the fact that "either
or" is more palatable than "yes or no."

The danger of this tool is that if used without tact and
finesse it seems like a gimmick and smacks of trickery.
Common politeness demands that if I am asking you for an
appointment, I should let you know that I am willing to see
you at your convenience — not mine. And unless I suggest
definite times, we do not arrive at any specific appointment.

An Intriguing Motivator

The ancient myth of Pandora and the box is an illustration of the effectiveness of curiosity as a motivator. Just as
curiosity caused Pandora to open that box, this same curiosity
has been opening doors ever since.

"Mr. Smith, other people in your line of work have found our product most beneficial. I'm sure you at least want to know how it has helped them."

"Our services brought an almost unbelievable savings to a company similar to yours. I can explain this great savings very easily and you can decide for yourself if you want this help also."

"The earnings of ABC company almost doubled when they took over this line. I can show this to you at your convenience and you can decide whether you are interested."

Benefits Not Features

There are two things that are particularly evident in the above remarks. Please note them both.

First, nothing is suggested about the details of the proposal (or product or service) itself. Without such information a prospect is not in a position either to accept or reject the idea. The communication is limited in scope. Only enough information is given to excite curiosity. This curiosity can only be satisfied through an appointment. This is very elementary, but too often we forget and tell too much about our product or service when seeking to sell the appointment.

Second, in the above efforts to set up an appointment, I offer only *benefits*. I am careful to steer away from *features*. This is done for several reasons.

Benefits excite curiosity much quicker and with greater certainty than features. The end results — the benefits — are always attractive. We can always relate ourselves to benefits, not always to features.

Also, if we speak only of benefits there is nothing for our respondent to reject. No one wants to refuse benefits to him. However, it would be different had I spoken of features in seeking to set up an appointment. Then there would have been something to consider in the line of comparisons. If I had said that I wanted an appointment to show a new type of inexpensive insulator, my respondent would now have information on which to decide against the appointment. He might say that his company had just laid in a big supply of insulators. He might say that they had already tested other brands and were satisfied with what they had. He might even question the inexpensive aspect of my approach and say that they had checked all prices and felt sure that their prices were right.

I am certain you see the value, when setting up an appointment, of arousing curiosity through only a brief communication of benefits.

The Great Difference

Many people do not realize that there is a great difference between an appointment and an interview. When we have gained an appointment, we have only received permission to go into the physical presence of our prospect — nothing more.

After we are in his physical presence, if we can then get into his presence mentally, that is, gain a reasonable amount of his attention and interest, we can say that we have an interview. We have emphasized this elsewhere in this book and we emphasize it again.

Please, *please* have the courage to walk away from an appointment if you can't get an interview. Be careful in your observation. If the body communication as well as the verbal communication by your respondent tells you that he has not given you a true interview, and if it becomes clear that you cannot at that time get the attention and interest you require for an interview, be professional enough to excuse yourself and leave.

Earlier in this book I have given you language that you can use. If you are tactful, your respondent will not be offended. After all, it is he who has refused the interview — not you. But don't waste your time!

Appointment Vs. Interview

A truly accomplished person in the field of communication always considers the appointment and interview as two entirely independent procedures. They are two distinct and different steps that must never be confused.

Some people never divorce or separate the two. These people are destined for great disenchantment in the field of dealing with others.

The Presentation

In the anatomy of persuasion it is, of course, unthinkable to consider the presentation until we have gotten through both the appointment and the interview. After we are in both the physical and mental presence of our respondent, we are ready to present the merits of our proposal. During this presentation we reach another plateau.

The appointment brought us into the physical presence of our respondent. The interview brought us into his mental presence through the attention and interest we gained. Now in our presentation we go from this mental presence into his emotional presence so that we can get action.

Since this chapter is primarily a review of principles we meet in a day's communication, I want to emphasize a few additional points on which we should concentrate.

Profitable Difficulty

I have had people differ with me violently when I have emphasized in my seminars, as I have emphasized and repeated throughout this book, that fear, apprehension and difficulty are to be welcomed by the ambitious person if he wants to continue in his growth.

Nature has a storehouse of riches for us all, but she only gives us those strengths which we need, when we need them, to meet and overcome the difficulties we meet in life. And so, since we only grow strong through adversity, there is a certain blessing we find in the obstacles we meet in our lives.

A very dear friend of mine who is truly a spiritual person seems to rise above any difficulty — and she has had many. I have known her for many years. At one time she complained a great deal. After her husband died, leaving her with four children, she felt as though she were a martyr. So persistent was she in telling her troubles that she was avoided by most of her acquaintances.

However, as other difficulties faced her over the years, she began to get stronger and to grow with each disappointment and seemingly insurmountable obstacle. Now she is truly a great person. Her indomitable spirit is an inspiration to all who know her. She spends much of her time comforting other people who perhaps are materially more fortunate than she but not as strong spiritually. Her compassion and interest in others has constantly grown as she has overcome each obstacle. Each stumbling block has only turned out to be a stepping stone for this great person.

The Blessings of Being Sensitive

Many people who do research and who teach in the field of human engineering embrace the theory that unless a person is sensitive enough to experience a definite fear when he is approaching people who might refuse his proposal, product or service, he will never be successful in the art of persuading others. I definitely subscribe to this theory.

This belief is based on the fact that people are so complex that only a sensitive person can appreciate the many emotions, ambitions and aspirations that are harbored in the human brain. So please consider carefully this point of view. Weigh the facts carefully before you disagree.

I hope you go even further with me and subscribe to the fact that this sensitivity, even though it causes fear, is a blessing to be prized. Without it you will never be able to appreciate the feelings of other people; with it you have a great fear of refusal. I repeat that about the third time we receive a refusal of our proposal product or service, we consider it a rejection of ourselves.

The Twin Factors You Need to Win

I would be mentally dishonest if I said that you could ever rid yourself of feeling the pangs of this fear of rejection without also losing the priceless sensitivity which I hope is yours. The two go hand in hand. You cannot enjoy the benefits of sensitivity without paying the price of fear.

Insulation Against Rejection

While we cannot completely get rid of this fear of rejection, and frankly if we did we would destroy our sensitiveness, we can reduce its acuteness to some extent without losing its benefits.

Man has always feared the unknown. Once he was petrified by thunder and lightning primarily because he did not understand their cause. Now that we understand these things, although we still have a certain respect and fear, we are not driven into a panic.

Similarly, if we realize why we have this healthy fear when we face the unknown response of a respondent, this knowledge helps us reduce this fear to manageable proportions. The mere fact that we realize nature gave us this fear of the unknown as part of self-preservation reduces the fear to some extent.

Restoration a Necessity

Yes, I hope you agree with me that as good sensitive persuasive communicators we do not desire completely to get rid of this fear of refusal. As these refusals of our product or service mount, I hope you agree with me still further that they become in our own mind rejections of ourselves. It's human nature to take this attitude. These rejections take a real toll upon us. The emotional trauma, however small, wears us down even as drops of water might wear down the hardest of rocks.

To be worn down and discouraged is no serious matter. I have said over and over, "Courage is not getting rid of fear — it is learning to cope with it."

If you have agreed with me this far, then there is only one thing left for us to do. Realizing that this inevitable fear will take a toll upon us, we must adopt a method to build ourselves up constantly just as rapidly or even faster than refusals can tear us down. This is the real test of our survival in the field of selling ideas, products or services.

The Only Answer

While some consulting and research firms might disagree on what specific tools are best for rekindling the fires of enthusiasm, all now agree upon two aspects of this necessary phase of training and conditioning.

First, if a company wishes to raise the enthusiasm of its employees no continuing program of motivation can successfully be given by an outsider. From time to time a person can be brought into an organization to raise temporarily the morale of that organization. The emotions may soar to great heights, but since emotions are transitory, this rise is only temporary. Consequently the problem is to get each individual to adopt his own program and habit of regenerating his spirits periodically.

Continuous Motivation

The second aspect of motivation agreed upon by all is that unless the program of recharging the enthusuasm of a person is permanent and pursued constantly, it is of no lasting value — if indeed it is of any value at all.

Thus our efforts should be directed at building within each person himself a self-motivation program to counteract the toll which refusals are bound to have upon him, and making every effort to convince that person that this is a never-ending task of rebuilding.

The Master Secret

One might feel that some of the matters covered in this chapter are foreign to communication. This is not true. The entire field of human engineering, every facet of the people business, is so interwoven with good persuasive communication, verbal and non-verbal, that one is blended with the other.

Put great importance on good communication in any and every field of your endeavors. You will never contribute to any great project, industry, business, or profession if you are not accomplished in communication. We cannot stress too strongly that the person who can't communicate his knowledge, regardless of the amount of knowledge or in what field it may lie, is no better off than the person who has no knowledge.

This is the Lifetime Plan I mentioned. It includes developing a positive mental attitude, sensitivity to the needs and wants of others, avoidance of being a victim, and self-motivation. These easily cultivated habits and attitudes can help you use *Kinesics* and the power of Silent Command many times more effectively. No matter what activity you're engaged in during the day, keep your eyes and ears open! Day by day, week by week, year by year, you will feel this incredible power build up in you!

SEVENTEEN

The Kinesics of Courtship and Romance

Nature intends to perpetuate each species of living thing, and uses courtship and sex as the instruments of this perpetuation. You can be sure, therefore, that all of us are generously provided with instinctive persuasive powers in this field. Almost unconsciously, men use their strongest powers of persuasive communication to attract women, and women use theirs to attract men. You can learn a lot about persuasive communication by observing the ways people use it to attract the opposite sex. The words people use in courtship, romance, and sex, and their non-verbal communications — using their bodies, color and style of clothing, jewelry and perfume — can tell you valuable things about how to be persuasive.

Men who are successful in wooing women often use many of the ways of persuasion described in the earlier chapters of this book. They also apply the lessons they learn in courtship to persuading their bosses and fellow-workers in business. Women in business know they must be attractive to others, not only to those in whom they might have a romantic interest. Both sexes must apply "courtship" to other types of relationships for persuasive communication.

One of the most successful career women I know is an officer in a large bank in the city where I live. This woman is handsome, charming, and immaculate in her dress. She is generously endowed by nature in her physical appearance.

Men enjoy transacting business with this woman, I am sure, as much because of her good looks as because of her business efficiency. She certainly capitalizes on her appearance, but never in a distasteful way. She has learned to apply persuasive communication in all relationships.

Courtship Signals in Animals and Men

The preening conduct of a bird, or the courtship dance of an animal, is designed to get the attention of the opposite sex. Human beings, too, have their own versions of a courtship dance for the same reason. It is a powerful attempt at persuasive communication, generally without words.

Such an attempt doesn't have to be an obvious approach or a noticeable demonstration. Suppose that several women are dining in a room alone. Several men come in and take a table nearby. Chances are more than likely that these women will take action that corresponds to the preening conduct of the birds. They will re-adjust their hair, fix their lipstick, and change the position of their bodies. One or two may excuse themselves to go to the powder room and primp there. In any event, "preening" steps will take place.

Likewise, let's suppose that four men are on the first tee of a golf course ready to tee off. Several very charming ladies who are strolling by stop to watch the performance. Do you think for a moment these men will conduct themselves in the same manner as they would if they were not being watched? The "strutting" and the "preening" will take place just as certainly as it did with the women except that it will express itself in a different manner. Each man is consciously on stage and puts forth special effort to make an impression.

Do you think that a small boy who pulls a little girl's long curls desires to hurt her? In reality he only wants to persuade her to notice him. It's his way of communicating the fact that he must not be ignored. At other times he'll hang by his knees or climb a tall tree because there are girls watching. This is simply his way of "preening." He attracts the attention of the opposite sex in the only way he knows how.

Using the Power of Sex Communication

On first impression it might appear that sex communication has only a limited function. Actually sexual attraction permeates practically every field of our private, our social, and our economic lives. It is widely used in advertising. The light-headed little girl on TV "with a body by Fisher and a brain by Tinkertoy" commands our attention for even the most uninteresting subjects. Have you noticed how many TV stations have employed such girls to telecast weather reports? And these types of sex communicators sell products. Many girls even try to imitate the Mae West "Come up and see me some time" style while giving the features and benefits of an automobile or house appliance.

Such use of sexy tones and manners to promote products annoys some people, but let's face it! Sex is here to stay. Love, as they say, may make the world go round, but sex keeps it populated. We must not ignore the power of sex when we study persuasive communication.

Communication by Dress

Just as the decor of a person's home reflects the personality of the owner, a person's dress and appearance communicate much to us about that person.

Consider these two extremes. A man is walking down the street in a black suit with a collar turned around. A moment later a young man, barefooted, long-haired, saunters down the same street. These two attires clearly communicate two different and distinct personalities, persuading us in different ways.

I am at a party and notice a young girl with a good figure. Her dress is cut low and seems even lower because the top button is unbuttoned. I don't have to tell you that the most carefully planned thing is a careless and accidental top button left open. I can't recall ever seeing this carelessness on the part of a woman who is not blessed with a full bosom. I suppose a flat-chested girl is by nature more careful and meticulous in her dress. She doesn't forget this top button. Nature gives her a better memory perhaps.

Does anyone doubt what the girl with the good figure is communicating?

> Nature endowed me generously and I am proud of it. I want to show as much of myself as I can without appearing to be a floozy. The best way to do this is to pretend that I accidentally am revealing more of myself than I intend to do. You cannot hold me responsible for my mistake. When you stare at that portion of my body, I am complimented. But I look away when you do it for fear that you might know that I am conscious of what you are doing. Please continue to stare at me.

Just as a matter of interest to you, the next time you go to a party carefully notice the attire of those who are there. Based on your knowledge of the people there, ask yourself if their dress is not designed to persuade in different ways.

Color Communicating

The personality of an individual is often revealed by the colors adopted in his or her home and by the colors preferred in clothing. It has been said that bright colors are worn by an extrovert and more conservative colors by an introvert. To some extent this is true, but since brighter colors have become more popular in all dress we might be misled if we accepted this principle too literally.

In past years we have associated red, purple, and the heavier colors with an invitation for sex participation. I am sure that we cannot assume in our modern times that any color, in and of itself, expresses this. However, we all certainly will agree that certain bright colors will encourage the making of "advances" more than will subdued colors.

How would you feel if you went to a funeral and saw some female relative of the deceased wearing a loud red coat and a matching red dress? Certainly this color would not signify sorrow and deep respect on the part of that person. Red is a motivating color, one that brings stimulation and action, and is not suitable for the occasion.

A person wearing green on St. Patrick's day is communicating for sure. Likewise a red, white and blue dress worn on the Fourth of July certainly tells us something. The Christmas spirit is apparent in a person who wears red on December 25th. That person is communicating happiness, joy and good will to all mankind.

Persuasion Through Odor

No treatment of non-verbal communication is complete without at least a reference to odor.

Among animals the scent is perhaps the one most important factor in identity, invitation and response. We only have to observe animals to be convinced of this. It seems to be one of nature's miracles that a new-born calf and its mother can identify each other among a thousand cows and calves by mere scent.

An eligible young lady in many cases will go without food before she will deprive herself of a tantalizing perfume. If a man who is particularly attractive to a girl compliments her on a certain kind of perfume, what perfume do you think she will use when he next dates her? The persuasive effect of perfume in many cases brings a man to the emotional point of popping the question.

Most people claim that odor will bring back fond memories of things that happened years ago quicker and more vividly than anything else. I never smell roses without having my memory carry me back to my childhood days when I picked roses from our yard and carried them to my teacher. The communication is quick and vivid and sentimental.

I know a certain real estate person who always asks the owner of a house he is showing to put on the coffee pot before he brings the prospect out for inspection. He told me that nothing communicates comfort, relaxation and domestic atmosphere as vividly as the smell of coffee.

Using Eye Communication

Among the numerous ways that we communicate with our eyes none are more carefully planned than when we are trying to persuade the opposite sex. We use our eyes in different ways and in varying intensity.

It is true that many people have eyes which are more expressive than others. But I am sure that it would be difficult to find anyone who does not communicate to some degree with his eyes.

We have been told from childhood, "Don't stare." In most cases this is good advice. Staring is rude because it makes the object of our stare uncomfortable.

However, there are exceptions to this rule. For instance, a man stares admiringly as a beauty contestant walks by. His stare communicates, "You are a gorgeous creature. How wonderful it is to radiate such beauty. You make the world a nicer place in which to live because there are such people as you".

No woman resents a stare of admiration. If the stare, however, goes beyond admiration and has the leer of anticipation and desire for possession it makes many women uncomfortable.

The Come-Hither Look

A friendly glance by a person, accompanied by a smile, often communicates to either sex that he or she likes people and would enjoy a conversation. Such an attempt at persuasion is more likely to happen when one is on a plane, waiting in a reception room, at a social function or the like. Such occasions offer a natural climate for this type of experience.

Don't expect such a persuasive glance and smile to have this effect in a crowded elevator or walking down a busy street. If you attempt such a communication under the wrong circumstances you are certain to be embarrassed.

Remember that there are varying degrees of eye communication. A man often conveys the message to a girl, "May I join you?" simply by opening his eyes wider than usual and even slightly raising his eyebrows. I have seen this same inquiry made by simply squinting the eyes.

It depends a great deal on the circumstances and location. A wink has always been interpreted as an invitation. If a person looks into the eyes of a person beyond the usual second or two, he or she is usually inviting a response. This is in most instances considered the safest way to make an approach because it gives one a method of saving his ego if he doesn't get a favorable response.

The "I Am Willing" Stare

If the other party is congenial to a meeting, all he or she has to do is continue to stare back. This is articulate communication and implies that "I too, would like to make our relationship more intimate. You are permitted to accost me. I shall not be insulted. I shall not rebuff you or shatter your ego."

This staring back does not, however, communicate anything other than the preliminary meeting. In salesmanship, it is called "selling the appointment."

The Extent of Intimacy

If a man staring at a girl finds that she glances away before permitting enough time to elapse to commit herself, he can easily save his ego. He does not undergo the embarrassment of feeling that he was rejected. He too can glance away as though he never intended to send a message or offer an invitation.

The stare approach is complete insurance against a shattered ego. This is not true in many other methods of inviting a more intimate relationship. For instance, if a man asked a woman if he could join her and she raised her chin as though she were highly insulted and turned away, how could he save his ego by claiming that she misinterpreted his intent, that he never requested permission to join her?

It is amazing and almost unbelievable to find out the extent of intimacy which a man can reach with a woman as long as he constantly communicates to her "I still consider you to be a perfect lady." He may do this without speaking, as evidenced by the following reactions:

"He looked at me so adoringly, how could I resist?"

"I could tell by his expression that he was serious about me."

"His big brown watery eyes, fixed on me so lovingly, convinced me that this was not just temporary with him. That's why I consented, if you must know why!"

"He reached up with his arms in such a sincere pleading way, no woman could resist."

Everyone has a self-image which he or she must preserve. We can call it our self-respect or even our pride. It is important to us all that we maintain this. Actually what we think of ourselves is in reality more important than what other people think of us. The rule that you must persuade the other person you continue to respect him holds in other relations just as it does in courtship. Both men and women fear loss of respect, and will react coldly if your "look" indicates a lack of respect.

This principle of permitting the other party to save face is something we should remember in all facets of our dealings with other people.

A girl recently rushed up to me at an airport, thinking that I was someone else, and greeted me enthusiastically. When she realized that we had never met before she was greatly embarrassed. Seeing her plight, I said, "You look so familiar to me, too. I am *sure* we must have met somewhere."

Her embarrassment left her immediately and we laughed about the incident when it appeared to her that we both were mistaken.

Occasions are offered frequently where we can help the other party save face. All of us, I am sure, have read about the genial host, one of whose guests knocked over a glass of water and felt humiliated. The host made a point of doing the same thing twice before the evening was over. His guest soon gained his poise and even felt a little sorry for the host.

The most persuasive and successful "eye communicator" is one who conveys in his look that he is always willing to help the other person save face.

How to Make an Appointment with Your Eyes

One of the first lessons taught any new salesman is that the sale of the appointment should never be confused or mixed in with the sale of the product or service. His first task is to sell his prospect on just the importance of listening. Eye communication is mainly devoted to "selling the appointment."

The new salesman is even impressed with this fact: "It is easier to sell a person who isn't interested, if you can get the appointment, than to find a person who is interested."

Communication by Voice Pitch

Does anyone doubt that the low guttural voice of a Charles Boyer is a sex symbol? People today speak of a sexy voice just as they would speak of a sexy figure.

A high school teacher friend of mine was attending a teachers' conference. The first morning her eyes were caught by the intent and steady gaze of a handsome man, a tall and athletic fellow-teacher. My friend confessed that she had difficulty concentrating on her school work that day. Twice she found herself in a trance. She kept daydreaming of his stare.

"What shall I wear tonight to catch his attention?" she kept asking herself. She decided to wear a somewhat daring dress.

That night at the reception she appeared a little late, in her shortest and tightest dress, a rather low cut, black outfit. She wore her hair in an upswept style with her ears clearly showing and graced with long dangling earrings. I am sure that her appearance communicated in a loud voice, "I am delightful and available if you know how to make the right approach."

As she entered the reception hall, the first person she spotted was the handsome stranger, immaculately dressed and apparently waiting for her. At close range their eyes met again. Then she was shocked to hear a high, squeaky voice say, "May I sit with you for awhile?"

My friend told me she excused herself quickly. She was suddenly the victim of a headache, turned in early, and spent the evening with her books. Never in her life, she said, had she built her hopes up to such a disappointing let-down.

Actually, if my friend was really as anxious to meet the "right person" as she indicated she was, she should have waited to see if she could get him to drop his voice a half-octave or so. She put disproportionate importance on the pitch of his voice.

Nevertheless, this example shows how others may judge us, to our detriment, by the sound of our voices. As in courtship, so in other situations must we be sure our voices help us to persuade. We should all take inventory of our vocal personalities from time to time. What does the tone of your voice communicate to others?

I present a "voice clinic" once a year, and urge everyone who attends to purchase a small cassette tape recorder and bring it to the clinic. The first day we have those who are attending record a neutral message such as the alphabet or the multiplication table, in a tone that suggests either sex, pride, fear, surprise or other emotion. When each person has done this, others are asked to interpret the emotion when it is played back. Those who do not clearly communicate the emotion they intend are coached until they can do so. With the help of friends, you can develop this skill yourself.

Body Position

The position in which one stands and sits can give a persuasive message, according to all researchers and writers on this subject.

How does the strong, silent "sex symbol" of the movies

stand? Does he stand as though he were a soldier in the presence of an officer? No, he has a casual, sophisticated slouch. He throws out one hip as though it were almost out of joint. More weight is put on one leg than on the other, which is carelessly crossed over in front of him. A hand on one hip even helps to build the image.

This man is communicating, "I am a man of the world. I am sure of myself. I am relaxed and confident. It's not necessary for me to be eager or disturbed about the future — I don't have to be."

The average woman communicates more articulately with her standing position than a man. She has more to communicate with, and a woman's body is more flexible and lends itself to body language better.

The next time you see a group of women sitting together without any men near, just study their positions and manner of posture. Notice how the same women hold themselves and act while sitting in the presence of men. You can see that they neither sit in the same position nor act the same.

You might ask if this ability to distinguish the difference has any value. It has this value. If you wish to become experts in the field of persuasive communication, you must observe and study every facet of such expressions. We cannot be accomplished in one type of body communication without understanding such communication in its entirety.

You must remember that the meaning of a particular action depends upon time and place. If a woman is sitting in a bar alone at midnight and leans over to a man on the next stool and asks for a light, do you think she has a right to make this man feel that she has been insulted if he propositions her?

The time, place, and circumstances have much to do with interpreting the communication of certain acts or movements. If this same woman asks this same man for a match while they are both waiting in line for a plane ticket in a busy terminal, we have a right to draw entirely different conclusions from her actions.

The Language of Sexual Communication

It is well to understand the language of sexual communication, even though you may have no desire to send out sexual invitations, or interest in responding to such invitations. Your knowledge of persuasive communications, particularly non-verbal communications, will be increased if you observe the sexual communications of others, and to do this, you must truly learn to "listen with your eyes."

Look at the clothing people wear, their choice of colors and scents, the way in which they move their bodies and stare at others. People are becoming far more outspoken in bodily sexual communication than in the past. Study courtship and "preening" to learn which communications are persuasive and which are not. Maybe you yourself have been unconsciously sending out wrong messages to others.

EIGHTEEN

The Rewards of
Silent Command

There are two balance sheets to every company. One is handled in the accounting department; the other, which might be called an "invisible balance sheet," is found in the personnel department. The first reflects the financial strength of the company. The second reflects the people strength of that company.

Which is more important is too obvious to need elaboration. If we wiped out all the physical assets of du Pont today, in perhaps a year's time these assets would be replaced and the company would be back in business. However, if all personnel were wiped out, there would likely be no du Pont Company ever again.

A Great Inventor's Secret

One of the most vital factors affecting this invisible balance sheet is the ability of a company to communicate. This communication within the company, as I stated before, is on a horizontal basis between employee and employee and on a vertical basis between supervisor and employee. Also we must consider communication with the public in building a public image.

This opportunity of building better communication is never ending. It can always be improved. As the great Thomas Edison said, "There is a better way to do it — find it."

An Action Plan for Daily Living

I once heard a third-day convention speaker utter a prayer: "Dear Lord, bless the speakers on the first day of a convention. Their listeners are fresh and full of intellectual curiosity. They have an opportunity to stir emotionally and stimulate mentally. Their opportunity is great — they are indeed fortunate.

"Also, dear Lord, bless and help the speakers on the second day. Their listeners are becoming tired and disinterested. These speakers need help; they are faced with a real problem.

"But as for any speaker on the third day of a convention, dear Lord, please have mercy on his soul."

I personally differ in this philosophy. I always prefer to be the last speaker at any convention. This is the time when those attending should pause, take inventory of what they have learned and resolve to do something about it. Nothing is more useless than knowledge which is not put into use; nothing is more powerful than knowledge put into action.

For the same reason I feel that the last chapter of this book is by far the most important.

I hope you will consider the communication ideas and principles covered in this book and give much thought and consideration to the manner in which you are going to adapt them to your work and everyday living.

How to Get Help When You Need It

One of the reasons why many people fail to use good ideas received from a book is that they try to absorb too many ideas on first exposure. This book is designed to be a reference book and also, hopefully, an enjoyable book.

After the first reading don't try to put into use more than one or two ideas. Don't try to remember too many things you read. Unless an idea is so good that it embraces you rather than being embraced by you, chances are that you will not remember it anyway. So on first reading pick out one or two ideas that reached out to you and then *start using them.*

Since this is a reference book, I hope you will refer to it many, many times. After one idea has become a part of you through constant use, go back and read again with the idea of taking another idea that appeals to you and putting that idea into use also.

Above all else please remember that to put one idea into use is far more beneficial than mentally to absorb a hundred ideas which you simply "pigeon-hole" away in your brain. I am sure you have realized while reading this book that my primary effort has been not to clutter your brain with numerous communication ideas but rather to encourage you in procedure which will enable you to use to best advantage the simple rules of good communication known to us all.

The one test of whether this book was worth my writing and worth your reading is found in this question, "Are you going to be better in your work for having read this book?" Unless you put at least one idea contained in this book into action, the answer to this question is "No."

In order to help you in your thinking as to whether this book will have any lasting effect upon you, I shall offer a few suggestions regarding your possible future action.

How to Prepare for the Future

First, do you have a strong desire to prepare yourself for more effective communication in the future? Do you really *want* to grow in strength so that you can compete in an increasingly competitive world? Do you have a compulsion to perfect your persuasive powers?

Don't be impulsive in your decision; don't consider this question lightly. Be honest with yourself. Not everyone has this desire. Many are satisfied to sit on life's sidelines and just watch the success parade go by. They not only lack any desire to lead the parade, but they don't even care to be in the parade. They are perfectly satisfied to be spectators and merely watch others march ahead.

Some people have built-in limitations; they prefer a life of quiet desperation; they are allergic to effort; they don't even burn the candle at one end. I've known people who started at the bottom of the ladder and simply found it more comfortable to remain there than to attempt to climb up rung by rung. They fall into that great category of people who prefer to endure the deprivations of failure rather than make the sacrifices of success. Of course, this is their privilege.

The Two-Edged Sword

We are all born free and equal in our right to fail as well as to succeed. Otherwise, we would not be living in a democracy.

Do you realize that the Constitution of the United States of America, the Bill of Rights, even the ancient Magna Charta, all guarantee to me that I have the right to fail as well as to succeed? This is the very essence of democracy. It is a two-edged sword, and it's up to me and me alone to choose which edge I shall use to carve out my future. I might tell you that I am a totally worthless individual, that I am absolutely unmotivated by anything, and furthermore, that I like it that way. My friend, this is no concern of yours. I am sure you would not admire me; I am positive you would not consider me a candidate for distinction; but disgusting as I might appear to you, you must respect my right to follow this formula for certain failure if I so desire.

I repeat the first question, do you have a strong desire to prepare yourself for the future?

The Second Question

The second question is of far greater importance. Even if you are sure you have the desire, is this desire strong enough and compulsive enough to cause you to do something about it? Are you sure you are willing to do certain things *now*, whether you enjoy doing them or not, which will lead with certainty to future happiness and success?

Man throughout all history, in all ages and in all lands, has been plagued with this great choice. Does he want to gratify his immediate impulse or does he want to accomplish his ultimate purpose? This choice is yours at this time. Be honest with yourself. If for some reason you cannot answer these two questions in the affirmative, if for some reason your thirst for success is not enough to make you willing to undergo certain sacrifices, I say that you should abandon this book at once. It has nothing of help for you. But if, on the other hand, you desire your just share of the tasks and rewards of this life, and furthermore, if you want them enough to make some temporary sacrifices in order to obtain them, then this book can be the road map to the great city of your dreams, your ambitions, and your aspirations.

Every individual has within himself the seeds of his own growth and the virus of his own destruction. Whether he cultivates a condition for growth, or whether he creates a climate for destruction depends upon his decision regarding these two important questions. To answer the first question is not enough; your decision must be made on both. For your sake, I hope you make them both in the affirmative. I sincerely believe that you have the strength, the ambition, and the self-discipline to do so, or you would not have read this book to its final chapter. I hope that I am right.

The Amazing Rewards of Silent Command

If you are willing to spend just five minutes a day to learn the principles of Kinesics and Silent Command, as set forth in this book, the doors of opportunity will swing open for you. The good things of life will be yours for the asking, whether you want money, power over others, devoted friends, a respectful and obedient family, passionate romances with the opposite sex, the admiration of your neighbors, community leadership, or anything else. These are the rewards you can expect — and win — if you master and use the techniques in this book.

The Greatest Gift

And, while I don't want to sound like a "Johnny-one-note" or a broken record, I repeat, "Unless you really want to succeed in this life, unless you earnestly want to better yourselves, unless you sincerely want a greater share of the good things in this world, want them enough to do something about it now, you should forget about this book at this moment because nothing I can say, in fact nothing that anyone else can say, will help your tragic and hopeless situation in life."

Yes, we "gotta wanna." We must have the gift of dissatisfaction. We must want circumstances to be better than they now are. If we are completely satisfied with our present state of life, and with everything that surrounds us, the pilgrimage has ended for us and we have already settled in our little city of compromise. It is only through divine discontent that we keep moving forward.

Yes, we "gotta wanna." Needs are not enough; wants are the magic ingredients. Wants alone bring out the best within us, not needs.

We are not, and probably never will be, a needy people. Needs are too basic and logical, and they push us only while we are in the realm of desperation. Wants are emotional, inspirational, sentimental, and lift us to new levels of accomplishment.

The Magic Formula

If we want certain things in life badly enough, we automatically draw upon those resources within us and convert them to productivity. We might have needed certain things for a long time, but until we finally begin to want them, we shall certainly never get them, unless by accident. Many people who merely need things sit idly by and dream of the joys they will experience when their dreamship comes in. This is the only sure way of "missing the boat."

Some people reading this book might say, "Why shout the obvious? I realize that in a world of changing values, shifting methods, and increasing competition, I must constantly be improving myself by learning more effective communication and adjusting to meet these new challenges. Be specific, spell it out, don't deal in vague generalities; tell me exactly just what I can do. I feel that I am worth the investment and I am willing to invest whatever time, effort, and money necessary to keep pace with changing times."

If you belong to this group, I congratulate you, I salute you. I am happy for you. Furthermore, I will give you a directional compass in the form of a magic formula, which, if followed, will lead to the great city of your ambitions and aspirations. It is not complicated. And, it has the basic virtue of being certain in its results.

No Limits to Your Success

First, our preparation must be a constant process with no ending. It must be forever moving, never static. School is never out for the person who really wants to succeed. There is no saturation point. All economic research centers agree that because of the rapidly changing phases of our economy, the average person in any line of endeavor today, regardless of his particular field, must be retrained many times.

It is somewhat disenchanting, I know, to find that just as we learn one role in life we are suddenly called upon to play an entirely new part, unrehearsed, as the drama of life must go on either with us, or without us.

The Day of the Flying Clock

The constant demands of readjustment offer a challenge today that never existed before. No longer is preparation something that can be put in a drawer and forgotten about. Success itself has taken on a new definition. It might even be termed today the constant and continuing changes of our economic system. I must emphasize that success today is a journey, not a destination.

Furthermore, in making this trip the important thing is that we must be constantly moving forward — seeking the progressive realization of a predetermined goal. The speed of our progress is of minor importance. Of major importance is the direction in which we are moving and the fact that we are always moving forward. It takes patience, and patience is not an easy virtue. This is the day of the flying clock. The motto of many is "Hurry, worry, bury." We have instant coffee and instant tea, but there is no "quickie" in the field of human development. We don't explode into success; we grow into it. And our growth should never end. Any person who selects a goal in life which can be fully achieved, has already defined his own limitations. When we cease to grow, we begin to die.

Tennyson perhaps expressed the idea best in his description of Ulysses, wandering in search of knowledge, new places, and experience: "I am a part of all that I have met, yet all experience is an arch wherethrough gleams that untraveled world whose margin fades forever and forever as I move."

New Worlds to Conquer

Yes, I am sure you agree with me that regardless of how well-qualified a person may be to meet the rigors of life today, if he is lulled into a sense of false security that he needs no additional preparation for the future, that his journey can ever be ended, soon he will find that he is lost in the frustrations of medieval thinking. And so, first and foremost, we repeat over and over and over the principle that in order to keep pace with changing times, we must pursue a constant program of self-improvement, a never-ending journey into new fields of knowledge and communication.

How to Become a Leader

And now for the second principle in our formula for success, which I present in the form of a question: "Are we trying to change our circumstances in life without being willing to make the sacrifices to change ourselves? Are we looking for a better job without being willing to do a better job? Are we trying to build a future without being willing to build ourselves?"

When we have once embraced this great human law and have accepted it for all time, we will have simplified in some measure many of life's problems: *We cannot accomplish anything greater than that which we are.* The picture can be no greater than the artist, the statue than the sculptor, the book than the writer. Human laws, as we know, are just as certain as the laws of nature. Just as water cannot rise above its source, our accomplishments can be no greater than those qualities which have been instilled in us.

Since time began the world has been made up of two classes of people. There are those people who look for a position in life which is not too difficult for their capabilities. Then there are those ambitious, resourceful individuals who seek to improve and prepare themselves for greater positions and opportunities of life. Those who seek to find an easier way of life have always failed. Those who seek only to make themselves stronger to meet the difficulties of life are our leaders today. You can be one of them.

You Shall Be the Miracle

Two men were sent out with hacksaws to salvage the bottom of a boat for scrap iron. One returned dejectedly and said that the task was impossible. The iron was too hard for the saws. The other came back and requested a saw of stronger steel, saying that the saw was too soft.

Two ships went out into the oyster-bed area. One crew soon returned stating that the oysters which contained pearls were too deep for their diving gear. The other crew came back to port for new gear stating that the helmets were too weak for the depth they were required to go.

Henry Ford, the man who put America on wheels, finally decided in 1928 that he would abandon the Model T and come out with the Model A Ford. He produced a trial model and assigned the task of thorough study of the new model to two of his engineers. The first engineer reported that the engine was too strong for the body; the horsepower must be reduced. The second engineer reported that the body was too weak for the engine; the body must be strengthened. It is unnecessary to tell you which engineer became the head of the Engineering Department of Ford Motors.

Only the difficult offers a real challenge. Phillips Brooks crystallizes the principle in very beautiful language: "Do not pray for tasks equal to your powers; pray for powers equal to your tasks; then the doing of your work shall be no miracle, but you shall be the miracle."

The Secret of Lifelong Improvement

Yes, there is only one way to improve the work, and that is by improving the workman — only one way to insure a masterful production, and that is by inspiring the master. Edwin Markham, the great poet of our early century, expressed this truth beautifully when he said, "We are all blind until we see that in the human plan nothing is worth the making unless it makes the man. Why build these cities glorious, if man unbuilded goes? In vain we build the works unless the builder also grows."

And so doesn't it stand to reason that the only way a man can be sure of meeting the changing aspects of life today is to be willing to make sacrifices for this preparation? It is a sad commentary on our present society that many people are more concerned with what they *own* than with what they *are*. Don't you be one of them! Be willing to pay the price.

There is an old Chinese proverb that says; "Give a man a fish and he will eat for a day; teach him how to fish and you have satisfied his hunger for life."

Today Is Your Day!

And now for the third principle in our magic formula for success. Not only must we realize that preparation for life's tasks and opportunities is a continuing effort, not only must we be mindful that we can only build the future by building ourselves, but we must also accept the truth that unless we have the desire and the courage to start now, *today,* we have missed the boat. Opportunity has passed us by.

One of the unhappy circumstances of this life is that the world is full of well-meaning but misguided people who want to prepare for the future; in fact, they periodically vow emphatically that they want self-improvement enough to do something about it. Somehow they never get around to it. Unless we are willing to start this very moment, from this very room, we shall never do it.

There is no tomorrow; yesterday does not exist; today, this very moment, is the only theater in which we live. Now is our only existence; we only live in the present. I put this thought into a little poem. It made it easier for me to remember the importance of the present. Perhaps it will help you as well.

TODAY IS YOUR DAY

This is my day — I did not ask it,
But t'was given me — I'll surely grasp it.

Leap upon it with all my might,
Embrace it, love it, hold it tight.

Yesterday is but a cancelled check,
It'll not return at call or beck.

Tomorrow is just a promissory note.
On this I will not dream and gloat.

Today alone is legal tender,
To this I pledge my best to render.

Now is the only time we live,
To this I pledge my best to give.

How valuable is your time to you? Can you afford to wait to start this preparation? What are you doing to make time more valuable to you? Have you evaluated it in terms of the human equation?

Our time is too valuable to waste. Furthermore, we know there is no tomorrow. So unless we resolve with all the sincerity which we possess that we shall start this very moment to build for the future, I am afraid that tomorrow, next week, next year, ten years from now, honest as may be our intentions, we will still find ourselves in the wilderness of procrastination, still responding to the siren songs of complacency. Why can't we realize that there is no other way except by starting now?

The Supreme Challenge

How satisfied are we with our lives up to this point? If we could live that part over again, would we do it differently? Do you plan to continue in the same pattern? I believe that most people who claim to be self-made men, if they had the opportunity to do it over, would welcome outside help.

It is the duty of every person to search humbly, sincerely — yes, and even prayerfully — for his place in the divine pattern of things, the place where he can contribute and give his best. The world owes us nothing, but we owe ourselves and our family the duty to develop our God-given qualities to the ultimate. It is a great challenge, and not an easy one to meet. But it is up to us and to us alone to make our dreams come true, our plans come alive.

But some of us would rather settle into a rut called complacency than find our own rainbow. The temptation of procrastination can be a cancerous sore, infested with destruction of the future; a jailer of progress, the chains and shackles that hold us back from our dreams and ambitions.

But if you believe in yourself enough, and value the future enough to start a program of self-improvement now, I salute you. One of the characteristics of a successful man is that he is never too busy chopping wood to take time out to sharpen the axe. I hope you will realize that this self-improvement is not complete until you learn good communication.

Opportunity Is Everywhere

My friends, I urge you to enter the great, the challenging, and the exciting world of persuasive communication. Don't let life pass you by. It is a tragedy to see unfulfilled dreams, unrealized ambitions, doors of opportunity which have remained unopened so long that the hinges are actually rusty. The great sorrow of this life is no longer a man without an opportunity; it is opportunity begging to be embraced by man.

You Cannot Fail

Yes, if you are willing to start a continuous self-improvement program, if you realize that you can only improve future conditions by improving yourself, and most important of all, if you have the ambitions, the ability, and the courage to make an immediate decision to start now, I say that you already are a success although you may have to wait a short time for the fruits of success. I say that you are already wealthy, and some day you will have money to prove it. Fortified thus, you cannot, and I know you will not, fail.

What you can do you ought to do. What you ought to do, I am sure you can do. And what you can do and ought to do, by the grace of God, I know you will do.

Good luck, God bless you; I hope you decide to prepare for the future, because believe me, *you are worth the investment!*